Wandering the World

WANDERING THE WORLD

Experiences of an Adventure Traveler

PEGGY SIMONSEN

HOUNDSTOOTH
PRESS

WANDERING THE WORLD
Experiences of an Adventure Traveler

ISBN   978-1-5445-1746-9 *Paperback*
          978-1-5445-1747-6 *Ebook*

*This book is dedicated to the memory of my parents,
who instilled in me a love of nature, and my husband,
Bill, who encouraged my adventurous spirit.*

CONTENTS

INTRODUCTION

Sailing along the coast of Antarctica in Iceberg Alley was like being in a gallery of ice sculptures. Walking among the gentle chinstrap penguins on glaciers was like having thousands of pets at my feet. And sliding down a glacier on our butts made us feel like kids again. Visiting my seventh continent had been a longtime dream and goal I finally achieved, and my friend Richard, who had not been particularly excited about going, said afterward that it was the best trip he had ever been on!

If *you* could go anywhere in the world and have any kind of adventure, what would it be? How would you decide, besides cost, where you would go and what you would do? Would it be to follow an interest or do something daring you have never done before? Once there, would you just observe, or would you participate? I hope this collection of my experiences will inspire you to seek your own unique adventures at whatever level of active participation is comfortable—or maybe uncomfortable—for you and those with whom you travel. But if you don't travel, perhaps you can read this as an armchair traveler to expand your awareness and enjoyment of the world.

This book is not a travel guide but a collection of experiences because of how I travel and because of my unique observations. As I recall many of these experiences, they seem to fall into sometimes unusual categories, such as garbage. But most of the categories parallel my interests and modes of travel. I share them not because I expect other travelers to experience the same situations but to demonstrate the wide variety of sometimes fun, often amazing, and occasionally unpleasant happenings that occur with adventure travel.

All my adult life, I have been a traveler. For many years, I traveled for work domestically and internationally as well as for adventure. I am a skier and sailor, and while my husband was alive, we took winter vacations skiing and summer vacations sailing. We also backpacked, camped, and hiked. Since I retired in 2003 as a widow, I have upped my travel to exploring places in the world I have not been to, with different travel partners who shared my various interests and need for adventure.

I consider any travel an adventure but particularly find it so when I am actively involved in learning and doing in a new environment. Occasionally, I enjoy sitting on a beach or attending normal tourist sites, but most of the time, I am exploring new territory, actively participating in unique activities, and making friends with a few others who seek the same adventure. My chapters are not a list of places I have been (though I have visited more than sixty countries and forty-nine of our fifty states) but rather some unusual or personal observations that others who visit the same places might not notice or experience.

I was encouraged to write this book by friends and family

who have read the Christmas letter with a photo page I have sent each year for many years, describing my travels and ventures that year. So I followed their suggestions and compiled a lifetime of travel adventures into this book.

I hope reading it inspires you to new quests or perhaps to revisiting your past experiences with new eyes. Come sail with me!

Bon Voyage!

Peggy Simonsen

"Life is my college. May I graduate well, and earn some honors."
—LOUISA MAY ALCOTT

Chapter 1

BOATS

"I must go down to the seas again, to the lonely sea and the sky,
And all I ask is a tall ship and a star to steer her by..."

—JOHN MASEFIELD

I'm starting this book with a chapter on boats because that
has been my preferred mode of travel and adventure. From
excursion ships to kayaks and most every type in between,
I don't count a trip complete without at least a tour boat on
the water at some point. I like to travel *in* boats, not *on* them.
For example, I am happiest in a Zodiac, close to the water
and wildlife, or in a kayak, managing my own path through
the water, and especially in a small sailboat, maybe diving
off to snorkel. But I have also had wonderful experiences
on excursion ships in parts of the world where a small boat
couldn't or shouldn't go. As you will see later in this chapter, I am not a cruise ship person, traveling *on* the ship as
a traveling hotel.

I grew up living near White Bear Lake in Minnesota, the
"Land of 10,000 lakes." We played in the water all summer,
swimming, diving off rafts, and sailing little Sunfish boats

with the intent to tip them over in order to right them again. White Bear Lake was the town where the scows were designed and built, so sailing was just what we did. We also canoed and "gunnel-jumped," which is balancing on the edges (gunnels) with another person with the intent of bouncing the competitor off. In college, I earned my Water Safety Instructor (WSI) certificate and worked as a lifeguard and swimming instructor at a Girl Scout camp, at a camp in Maine, and at a beach near my house. And I monitored the beach in a rowboat, so I could get to any kid quickly who was going underwater.

As an adult living in Illinois and not near little lakes, sailing and being in or near the water became a goal of our vacations, and we finally owned a large enough sailboat to handle sailing and racing on Lake Michigan. The saying about sailing is, "Hours of boredom interspersed with moments of sheer terror!" But I don't experience either extreme; I find sailing challenging and also restful.

SAILBOATS

One of the first sailing vacations my husband and I took was to the British Virgin Islands with friends. We chartered a "bareboat," meaning we had the boat without a crew; we were the crew. It was a forty-foot Beneteau monohull with four cabins and heads (boat bathrooms). That was my first experience with snorkeling, and I loved it! This was in 1987, and the coral and tropical fish were spectacular. The Caribbean water was turquoise and clear, and the little atolls we anchored by were mostly uninhabited by humans except for the occasional few seen at a beach bar. One afternoon, we had to choose if we wanted conch or mutton for dinner.

Not a fan of conch, I ordered mutton only to see a little goat pulled across the floor of the bar, hung from a nearby tree, and slaughtered. I ate dinner on the boat that night! But we were hooked on warm-water sailing.

RACING

We also came home and bought a larger boat (C&C 38) to sail and race on Lake Michigan. We harbored in Waukegan, a suburb north of Chicago, and participated in buoy races plus the occasional distance race from Chicago to Waukegan (about twenty-eight miles) with a crew. My husband became an excellent racer, and I got good as a driver, where I could focus on steering the racing line while Bill was the tactician and oversaw the crew and all the sail changes.

It was obvious that the next trip to the Caribbean would be to race. One spring, we flew to Saint Martin to join the Heineken Race Week. We chartered a boat from the Moorings with friends from Illinois who were experienced racers.

We quickly found out that some of our competition were company teams on rented boats, for which they bought new sails. (Chartered boats tend to have functional sails, not high-tech racing sails.) They had team uniforms with their company names on them, and our ragtag crew just wore whatever shorts and T-shirts we had brought. Others were experienced ocean racers from the East Coast and Europe. The first race was from the Dutch side of the island (Sint Maarten) to the French side (Saint-Martin), with an obligatory party that evening. The second day was from the French side back to the Dutch side, with competition for the best party. The third day was around the whole island, and we were elated to beat the company boats! No one expected people from *Illinois* to win, for heaven's sake.

Over the years, we competed in the Chicago to Mackinac Race, which was started over one hundred years ago by the Chicago Yacht Club. It goes the full length of Lake Michigan, 333 miles as the crow flies. But one rarely can sail as the crow flies; the wind determines how straight a line you can hold. Depending on the size of the boat, it can take up to three days and nights, and the weather can be cooperative, but usually, it's a challenge. Lake Michigan is considered a bathtub for waves because it is long and narrow, and when the wind blows from the north over the whole fetch of the lake, the waves can be eight feet or more. They are choppy because they break off one shore, then bounce back to break on the opposite. In July, when the Mac race is held, there can be horrendous thunderstorms adding to the challenge. Boats have been dismasted, had their sails torn, and more seriously damaged.

For one race, Larry Ellison, Founder of Oracle, shipped his seventy-foot sailboat to Chicago for the Mac race and bragged that he was coming to sail the pond only to find out how challenging the lake can be. He ate his words, but he did have a respectable time with the rest of the "sleds" (seventy-foot boats). Milwaukee is not even a quarter of the way to Mackinac Island, but we were passed by the sleds (our boats were half that size), even though we started an hour earlier.

One year following the Mac race, we continued to sail in the North Channel of Lake Huron, exploring the Northwoods along the shores of Drummond and Manitoulin Islands. The islands are forested rocky shores with very few towns or other sailors. We had provisions on the boat, of course, but a special treat was from a local resident who made pies from fruit in her yard and sold them to sailors like us stopping at a local dock.

After my husband died, I kept our new sailboat (a Farr 395) and competed in another three Mac races as captain with a capable crew.

I was one of two female captains of over one hundred boats
in those races. One night before the race, my new crew
partied too hard at the Commodore's Party at the Chicago
Yacht Club only to face eight-foot waves from the north with
hangovers as we started out. The sick crew members were
miserable and weren't of much use as we crashed up and
down the waves. In all the Mac races, we had respectable
times, but one is happy to finish with the boat intact, or even
finish at all after forty-eight to fifty-six hours of grueling

work. I had a crew of eight, so four of us would be on duty while the others slept, except if we needed a sail change, which required more hands on deck, so sleep time was secondary to keeping the boat sailing as fast as possible. Of course, there was always a great party on Mackinac Island when we finally got there, with all the skippers waiting to hear finish times and rankings.

In the last race I skippered, our section had eight one-design boats, all Farr 395s, so the weight and sail sizes were identical. In 2006, before the race required tracking devices on the boats, we were expected to radio our location as we crossed the forty-fifth parallel, about even with the Sleeping Bear Dunes on the east shore of Lake Michigan. It was night, so we couldn't see other boats, but we could hear our competitors all call in about the same time. Shortly after that, a massive thunderstorm could be seen just north of where we were heading. The sky was lit up with lightning and crashing thunder. We were sailing with the 1,200-square-foot spinnaker on a starboard tack, meaning that the wind was coming from the east, and the sail was flying off the left side of the boat.

We knew when the storm hit, the wind could come suddenly in huge gusts from the west. If it hit the spinnaker, it could rip the $8,000 sail, dismast the boat, or worse. So we made the decision to take the spinnaker down and just sail with the jib, which could be dropped quickly if needed. We sailed without the spinnaker for about twenty minutes until we could see that the storm went north of us. That slower twenty minutes cost us the race with our competitors, who gambled that the wind wouldn't change, so they left their chutes up. However, boats that were caught in the storm north of us did have significant damage; some had to with-draw and get themselves to shore. We were okay with our cautious decision.

After one of the races, friends came up and joined me as we sailed from Mackinac Island east to Government Bay and then around the end of Michigan's Upper Peninsula to the North Channel. My sister and brother-in-law had bought a cabin on St. Joseph Island, Ontario, on the shore of Lake Huron. It was too shallow there for my boat, which drew close to eight feet, so we got a slip at the harbor at Hilton Beach, which is a short drive from their cabin. It was fun sailing our new forty-foot boat into the harbor, where they rarely see a racer like that.

After another race, we did this again, picking up my brother, sister-in-law, and nephew for a cruise down the North Chan-nel. My nephew had not had the experience of sailing a big boat and loved being on the helm. He was unhappy when we had to take the sails down and motor when the wind died. We built a fire onshore to grill our dinner when a huge rainstorm hit, and we had to dinghy back to the boat with our food, all of us soaked. A forty-foot boat does have a good cabin and galley (kitchen) to hold us all in comfort, but in this case, we all fit in with our wet gear.

EXPLORING THE WORLD BY SAILBOAT

We chartered boats in interesting parts of the world for many years. One January, we sailed in the Gulf of California off the coast of the Baja Peninsula, starting at the south end at Cabo San Lucas. We had chartered a catamaran, which doesn't sail into the winds well. They are better sailing at a ninety-degree angle to the wind. We had north winds, and our destinations were north, so we bobbed on the waves a lot. One day, it was so rough that we turned around and returned to our previous anchorage. We wore wet suits in the water but mostly watched the sea lions from the dinghy. On the way home, the workers at the airport were wearing leather jackets with fur collars because, for them, it was cold—below ninety degrees!

My first trip to Australia was for an international conference, where I was invited to speak. My husband went with me, as he had never been there either. The conference was in Port Douglas, which is just south of the rain forest and a few miles from the Great Barrier Reef, the largest in the world. After I presented at the conference, we motored out to the reef. Only chartered boats are allowed to go to the reef and must tie up to a platform so as not to damage the fragile coral of the reef with anchors.

We signed up for a "resort dive," for which they fit you with a tank and diving gear standing waist deep on a small platform, and you go down with a guide. I was an experienced snorkeler but never had scuba training. I told the guide that I float easily, so he put one weight on my belt, and we went down a rope anchored to the bottom about thirty feet down. I knew that if I let go, I would float to the surface, even with the weight of the tank on my back. My mask leaked immediately, so I was getting salt water in my eyes and nose. My mouthpiece didn't fit snugly, so I was swallowing salt water. Plus, my ears wouldn't clear. When I signaled to go up to get the gear better positioned, I didn't know that I was ending the dive. My husband was swimming down on the seafloor, having a grand time, and didn't know what happened to me. I took the tank off and snorkeled happily on the surface. The water there wasn't as crystal clear as in the Caribbean, but the reef at the time (in the late nineties) had lots of tropical fish to watch.

After the group surfaced, the supervisor heard me describing what had happened and asked me if I wanted to file a complaint against the guide. Apparently, he had other customers who were unhappy too. We considered taking scuba training at home but decided that the opportunity to dive was so rare that I was better off just taking every opportunity to snorkel, which I have done since.

A great trip was sailing off the coast of Australia with friends in the Whitsunday Islands, a mostly uninhabited national park. There is a strong tide there, sometimes stronger than the winds. Each morning, we determined our destination based on the tide, not the winds. We had the boat provisioned, had vodka and tomato juice for Bloody Marys but no Tabasco or other spices except salt and pepper. When we found a little harbor and a store, we went shopping. The closest thing we could find was salsa, so we had lumpy Bloody Marys. We explored the islands and white sand beaches, rarely seeing another boat.

While visiting my son in San Francisco, we rented a small C&C sailboat in Sausalito on the north edge of the San Francisco Bay for a day of sailing. It was warm and sunny with a slight breeze blowing. We were wearing T-shirts. The boat we owned at the time was a bit larger C&C, so we knew how it sailed. Our intent was to sail around Alcatraz Island in the middle of the bay, but as we got a ways from shore, suddenly we were in dense fog with a stiff breeze blowing in from the ocean. It hit us hard, and as we tried to lower the sail on the traveler—a track that allows the sail to move to reduce the wind pressure to keep the boat from heeling (tipping too much)—we found that the hardware on the traveler was frozen from all the salt water. We were all experienced sailors, so we could release the mainsail and still hold the boat on course, but we had to abandon our goal of getting to Alcatraz. We couldn't even see the island, let alone sail to it. Besides, we were cold with just light windbreakers to wear. We came about and headed back to shore, where we found bright sunshine and warm temperatures again. We learned about San Francisco Bay's unpredictable weather that day!

Saint Lucia is at the south end of the Windward Islands in the Caribbean. It is farther away from other islands in the chain, so you can't see your daily destination sailing between anchorages. This is different from the Virgin Islands, where the next destination is close enough that it is usually visible while sailing to it. We had a sailboard along for the first time. It's a large surfboard that you stand on, with a sail and boom to maneuver it in the wind. I had never tried one before, so in a protected harbor, I got on and managed to get up, sail a ways, and was proud of myself until I tried to come about (change direction to go back). Every time I tried to pull the sail across and quickly get myself to the other side, I crashed. Sail and me in the water. I kept getting back on, pulling the heavy sail full of water up and got moving. Unfortunately, every time I struggled to do so, I was still heading away from the mother ship. The guys on our sailboat were laughing at me and calling, "We'll pick you up in South America, Peggy!" Worn out from tugging the sail out of the water, I pulled it on the board and used that as a kickboard to get myself back across the harbor to the anchored sailboat, where friends were having cocktails and enjoying my fiasco.

While sailing south from Saint Lucia to Grenada, just north of South America, we could see the Southern Cross constellation for the first time while listening to Crosby, Stills, and Nash singing their hit song "Southern Cross." That continued to be Bill's favorite song.

Another wonderful experience in the Caribbean is the sunset. The ocean stretches out before you with no land to break the view, and the second the sun goes below the horizon, we would watch for the green flash. Apparently, the sun's rays light up the plankton on the surface of the ocean, and for a split second, there is a green glow, then it's gone.

Coming back to Saint Lucia after a week of sailing, we were staying in cabanas on the jungle hillside the night before we were to leave for the airport. Our whole group was in one of the rooms finishing off our residual alcohol, and I went back to our cabana early to get to bed. I left the door unlocked so Bill could come in later. When he did, he didn't know where the key was, so he just put the chain lock across the inside of the door, which didn't lock automatically. Just before dawn, we heard a crashing at the door, and a barefoot native Saint Lucian smashed through the door, slid across the slippery tile wet from rain, grabbed what he could off the table by the couch, and turned around and ran. By the time we realized what had happened and got up, the thief had disappeared into the jungle. The biggest loss to me was a briefcase full of a work project I had spent vacation time writing, and Bill's Day-Timer, with credit cards but no cash. Not much value to the thief, but I had to tell my client the equivalent of "the dog ate my homework!" We were able to call American Express and have all the cards canceled. Luckily, I had taken our airline tickets out of my briefcase in preparation for our flight and had cash in my purse that the thief hadn't found. We reported the theft to the Moorings, who called the local police. When the inspector came, Bill remarked that he looked like Inspector Clouseau from *The Pink Panther*, wearing shorts with a raincoat over his shoulders. In his broken English, he asked Bill how he felt about the theft, and Bill said, "I'm pissed off!" which got written into the report as "I piss off." So much for justice in a banana republic! There was no other follow-up to the theft.

On another trip, this time to Saint Bart's farther north in the Caribbean, we had chartered a forty-five-foot monohull with eight of us on the boat. We were anchored and took our dinghy to shore to explore Gustavia, the main town on the island. As we were walking along, one friend said, "We should probably get lunch before the eights get here." We didn't know what he meant until we turned around and saw a crowd of people getting off a cruise ship and filling the streets, all with the number 8 on their shirts, following a guide holding up a large "8" sign. Forever afterward, people from cruise ships have been "8s."

On one trip, when we started our cruise from Saint Martin, we sailed south to Antigua, then overnight to Saint Kitts and Nevis. In the night, we could see fires on Nevis ahead of us and wondered if the island was aflame. We learned later that the farmworkers burn off the sugar cane stalks right after they are harvested, and we were happy to find the island intact when we got into the harbor.

A wonderful place to snorkel is an area called "The Baths" on the island of Virgin Gorda in the British Virgin Islands. There are very large boulders (geologically called karsts) in the turquoise, clear, warm water with a white sand bottom. There is no coral, but it's a great, comfortable way to snorkel in calm water and watch the tropical fish. We anchored our sailboat offshore, jumped in, and swam to The Baths. I could do this for hours without tiring.

*** * *

Before Bill died, we had made reservations to sail in Belize with friends, so after his death, they encouraged me to come anyway. My son was staying with me after finishing his master's degree and while looking for a job, so we decided to go. Bill and I had tried to get both sons to sail with us, but they never had time off at the same time. It was great being on a sailboat in the tropics, but I sat on the deck with the wind in my eyes to blow my tears away.

Off the coast of Belize, there exists the second-largest barrier reef in the world. Belize is protected from the open ocean by the reef, but it still has brisk winds. We were told to bring wet suits because of the jellyfish in the water. On the first day of snorkeling, I wore my wet suit, but it was one hundred degrees even in the water, and the suit is rubber, so it's hot. The snorkeling was great, but the second day, I decided not to wear the wet suit. I learned my lesson. The jellyfish are so small and transparent that you can't see them in the water, but they found me! They went down the front of my swimsuit and started stinging me immediately. I bounded out of the water to the boat, where the provisions included a bottle of vinegar. There I was, pouring the vinegar down my suit to ease the stings. Vinegar is an acid, which counteracts the poison of the jellyfish. No vinegar-and-oil salad dressing that night!

One day on the coast of Belize, we dinghied out toward the reef and jumped into the water maybe fifty feet short to swim out the rest of the way. As I started swimming, I realized I was not making any headway. The tide and waves were so strong, even on the lee side of the reef, that I was being pushed back as fast as I swam forward. Realizing this was a losing proposition, I swam sideways to get behind some rocks for protection. I watched as the others, one of whom was a stronger swimmer than me, also give up trying to reach the reef and swam sideways to where I was. We learned to wait until the tide and wind weren't so strong to get ourselves to the reef. Snorkeling is most fun in calm water when you can forget about the surface challenges and just float, observing and marveling at the fish and coral.

Back on the sailboat, we found a school of dolphins playing in our wake, so we dropped the sails and idled as we got off the boat to swim with them. My son treaded water and looked a dolphin in the face with the enticing smile they seem to have. Great experience.

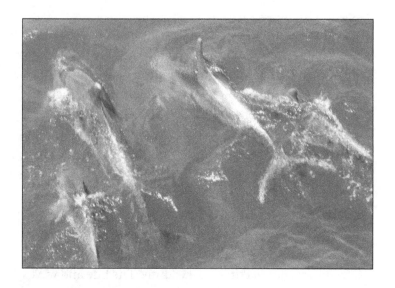

***

Some years later, I still had the strong desire to sail in far-flung destinations, so I chartered a boat from the Moorings in Tonga. Tonga is an island kingdom in the south Pacific Ocean. I managed to get both my sons, daughters-in-law, and granddaughter coordinated to join me for a week. We flew to Fiji and spent a couple of days in a lovely resort. On a whim, my friend Richard and I had the opportunity to go parasailing and were pulled over the ocean by a speedboat that goes fast enough to get us in the air. A unique adventure looking down from a couple hundred yards up until the boat slowed and we gradually dropped into the ocean.

I had given my granddaughter Libbe a mask, snorkel, and fins for Christmas in preparation for this trip in April. She was nine and had been taking swimming lessons in a pool but had no experience swimming in the ocean off a sailboat, so it was good to practice in the lagoons of the resort. She took to using the snorkel like a fish, as they say. Her swimming was good, but she hadn't yet incorporated the breathing, so having a snorkel, she just kept her head down and went for it. I was delighted! Then, when we got to Tonga, the first day on the boat, we stopped by an underwater cave and were getting ready to dive off and go exploring. Before any of us were ready, off jumped Libbe, with her gear on and swimming away. We had insisted on her wearing a life jacket always while on the boat, so that was reassuring, but her dad quickly jumped in and went after her. She certainly eased any concerns I had about being afraid of the deep water or the snorkel! Some of the islands in Tonga have quite a current around them, so while Libbe and I were exploring, she asked if she could hold my arm as we swam. I was glad to comply, keeping her nearby but not discouraging her sense of adventure.

We had mostly chartered monohulls, knowing how to sail them from our racing experience, and liked the handling and speed. We had chartered a monohull in Tonga. But after the week when we returned to the dock at the harbor, there was a big catamaran anchored on the other side of it. Both daughters-in-law went over to check it out and came back saying, "Next time, that's what we want." Catamarans sail flatter than monohulls, and have a large "salon," with a table and bench seats, so things don't need to be battened down like they do on monohulls, which heel on edge. Catamarans are more like a cabin on the water. I took note, and the next charter was a catamaran in the British Virgin Islands. Easy sailing and easier to live on for a week, but harder to sail into the wind. On the return to the harbor, we, of course, had headwinds and bounced up and down, not making much headway to get back by our check-in time. Cats (as the boats are called) usually draw less water (have a shallower keel) and can be sailed in shallower water than some monohulls. Pros and cons.

$$* * *$$

My most recent opportunity to sail on the ocean was in the Bahamas on a windjammer. I convinced my sister to join me. She is a sailor but is not as adventurous as I am, especially in the water. We got on the ship in Nassau, then sailed to the island of Eleuthera, a long, thin island with one side on the Atlantic and the other on the protected Caribbean. We had expected to sail to the Exumas, considered the "out islands," but the winds were strong, and the open ocean we needed to cross was rough, so the decision was made to reach protected Eleuthera instead and spend the week hopping to ports and small islands along the coast. The boat was a two-masted schooner, gaff-rigged (meaning the sails had a spar across the top rather than a triangular sail of sloop-rigged boats). It had twelve cabins for twenty-four passengers and a crew of eight. Not luxurious accommodations, but part of the adventure. Passengers were asked to help hoist the huge sails but, otherwise, could choose to do what we wanted while we sailed. We anchored by white sand beaches to have lunch onshore and snorkel in the turquoise water. Even though the Bahamas have the third-largest reef in the world, we didn't find much coral. The reef is more on the Atlantic side of the island chain, and the calm waters are on the lee side. While snorkeling, we did see lots of tropical fish and enjoyed warm, clear water and sandy beaches. All over the world, the coral is not as colorful as it was twenty and thirty years ago, as it is bleached from ocean acidification, which is caused by warming oceans. It is sad to see, but I am so glad I was able to snorkel some of the best reefs in the world back then.

We explored several little harbor towns and had great meals on the boat. On the rough passage from Nassau to Eleuthera on the first day and back on the last day, some passengers were seasick. However, over the years, I have learned that I am fine if I stay on deck and don't go into a small space, like our little cabins. I also have found a seasick medicine, Stugeron, that doesn't knock me out like Dramamine does. A windjammer (a clipper ship with passengers) was one more reason to get out onto the ocean, and with a friendly group of passengers, it was a great week.

Sailing on the ocean is exhilarating. Waves can be huge but usually are big rollers, so the boat rises and falls smoothly with the waves. Sailing on Lake Michigan with big waves is much choppier. Even a big boat can fall off the sharp crests of waves, slapping hard and jarring the boat and passengers. Steering in that kind of sea takes skill and concentration to try to steer at an angle to the crests of the waves. With a destination, sometimes it is not optimal to take a course at an angle to the waves instead of navigating directly into them. Whether in the Great Lakes or oceans, sailing is my favorite way to be on the water.

CANOES AND KAYAKS

Another favorite way to be on the water is in a kayak or canoe. As kids, we used to canoe in lakes in the Minnesota Northwoods, either just for fun or paddling while my dad fished.

In college, I worked on the waterfront in a Girl Scout camp in Northern Wisconsin, teaching swimming and canoeing, and took girls on canoe trips on the little lake. I still remember the overnight canoe trip I led with girls who had passed their waterfront tests. Coming back, we had headwinds and waves to battle, so it was hard going for eleven- and twelve-year-olds. We hugged the shore, making it longer but safer to get back to the camp. As an adult, I have had more experience in kayaks, and I like them better than canoes because of the maneuverability and ease for one paddler.

My husband loved to fish, so we spent a couple of summers at a fishing camp in Manitoba. We flew to Winnipeg, then took a puddle jumper plane to Kenora. The camp included several lakes around a large central lake. Each day, the owner asked what kind of fishing we wanted to do, then directed us to the appropriate lake. I am not a fisherperson and referred to this "catch and release" as "going out to torture fish for fun." But I was happy handling the canoe while Bill fished. Other days, we had a small motorboat to navigate to where the fish were biting. We did get to eat some good walleye (called "pickerel" in Canada), either for shore lunches or for dinner at the lodge.

Perhaps the least fun canoeing experience was in Northern Minnesota in Boundary Waters National Park. It's beautiful country, a massive area where you need to follow a map, so you don't get lost in the maze of islands. But the reason this experience was not fun was because of the blackflies! If you have ever been in the Northwoods in June, you know what I mean. They swarm and bite! It is hard to canoe *and* swat at the flies at the same time. A hat keeps them out of your hair, but they are in your face. When it's warm and you have exposed skin, they can make an otherwise great experience terrible.

* * *

Shortly after my husband died, I retired. While I was still grieving, friends invited me to join them in New Mexico for a kayak trip on the Colorado River south of the Hoover Dam. Tony was an expert kayaker, and in fact, he had built a very light kayak. We drove from New Mexico to a launch spot on the Colorado and put in three kayaks shortly after 1:00 p.m. Tony had the light one, which tipped over more easily; Bonnie had a one-person kayak; and I had the larger one, which was more stable and also carried our camping gear. Our plan was to paddle upriver to the base of the dam and find a camping spot. The current was strong, paddling was difficult, and we weren't making as much headway as planned. At one point, Bonnie lost her paddle, so we floated backward to grab it and had to retrace our distance again. We ended up short of our goal, found a camping spot with a hot spring to soak our tired muscles, and spent the night. We learned the next day that the dam releases water at 1:00 p.m., and it's the strongest current of the day, so we were battling that. We finished the trip more easily the second day and arrived as close to the dam as allowed. We walked over to explore the public sections of it. Since 9/11, they control access to the dam itself and keep boats away from the base of it. We paddled downstream in a couple of hours, which was the same distance it had taken us a day and a half to maneuver against the current.

Seeking any way to be on the water in a boat, I jumped at the chance to kayak in the Andaman Sea when visiting Thailand. We went from shore, paddled around a few islands with other kayakers, and stopped with our guide on a sandbar for a fresh-cut pineapple snack. Warm, blue water, calm sea, and sun! Great experience. I also kayaked in Mongolia on Lake Khuvsgul, a lake that borders Siberia. We were staying in a camp on the shore but had the opportunity to kayak on the calm lake for the afternoon, but not all the way to Siberia!

Another fun kayaking experience was on the Chicago River in the city. A group of us were able to take kayaks from the East Bank Club on the river and paddle through the middle of the city. We went up the north branch of the river, then out toward Lake Michigan under many of the bridges, and then down the south branch. It was a lovely, sunny day, and many of the people walking along the river called down to us and wondered how we could get kayaks on the river. It was fun and looked like it to onlookers. Leisurely paddling and looking at the view is a wonderful way to be in the middle of the spectacular architecture of the city.

* * *

After I met my friend Richard, the first trip we took together was to Alaska's Glacier Bay on a kayak adventure. We were on a trawler that held twelve passengers, and we kayaked daily in little inlets in the larger bay. Because the boat was small, we could poke into inlets and move alongshore, where large cruise ships couldn't go. The first time Richard and I were in a kayak together, it was a test of our new relationship! The trawler anchored a few hundred yards offshore, but the tide was going out, it was windy, and the water was wavy.

We got into the kayak with Richard steering, and immediately we were blown off course and luckily onto shore. Turns out, the kayaks had rudders run by pedals with the sternman's foot. Richard had kayaked in Mexico and Peru on mountain streams and was accustomed to using the rudder pedals like a gas pedal in a car—toe down to steer right and left. However, we discovered that these kayaks worked by pressing the whole foot down, heel included. Once he learned that, I stopped swearing, and we did fine.

Kayaking took us up close to calving glaciers. It was great fun to kayak to the base of glaciers that were calving (far enough away not to get swamped) and watch the huge chunks break off. While exciting to watch, when calves break off and float away, it shows that the glaciers are losing substantial volume, often caused by ice melting into cracks.

After a bracing exercise on the water each day, cocktail hour was fun with interesting comrades. The food was wonderful and included fresh-caught halibut and salmon for dinners prepared by the boat owner, who was also the chef. Our relationship survived!

One late afternoon we all got into a skiff and motored out into the bay, where the humpback whales were putting on a show. They circled our little boat and were jumping and breeching (diving with their tail flukes flapping) all around us. One of the passengers with us was an excellent photographer and captured some superb photos, which he sent to us after the trip.

* * *

Returning to the Northwoods, this time on Isle Royale National Park in Lake Superior, Richard and I had the fun experience of kayaking in the lagoon. We were able to glide quietly and watch the loons diving while listening to their crazy calls (source of the saying "crazy as a loon"). That is quite a different experience than paddling on Lake Superior, which can be very rough. Isle Royale is uninhabited except for a lodge on the shore, so while hiking or paddling, one is not likely to see anyone else. It's definitely a wilderness experience.

We also kayaked near the San Juan Islands off the coast of Washington. It's open ocean, but the islands are close enough together to provide protection from ocean swells and winds, so it's a great place to kayak. This was several years after the Alaska learning experience, so we got along and kayaked as a team, exploring and stopping for photos.

I also had a chance to kayak in Costa Rica in the lagoons. The trip with my friend Wendy, also an adventure traveler, was with a group called Adventure Women. We did all sorts of active things in Costa Rica (see the next section, "Whitewater Rafts"), but maybe the tamest was kayaking. It's fun to glide quietly through the mangroves and watch the water birds, nurse sharks, and alligators, which left us alone.

I have kayaked with my ski club (yes, we do summer activities too!) on rivers in Northern Illinois. We have varying levels of skill and run into varying levels of difficulty with fast water and a few rapids. The most common cause of turning over was being pushed sideways into branches or rocks, causing a quick hit and tipping the kayak. Once, a friend in another kayak and her partner tipped completely, dumping them and their gear into the water. She had a dry bag along with her phone and watch but didn't have it closed, so they both were ruined. They retrieved the cans of beer, but she had to borrow some dry clothes that I had brought along when we went onshore to lunch.

WHITEWATER RAFTS

The best rafting experience I have had was on the Colorado River in the Grand Canyon. On another trip with Adventure Women, we had sixteen women on two rafts with a guide. We covered about 180 miles, starting at Lee's Ferry at the north end of the canyon. We spent six days floating and navigating whitewater down to Havasu Creek. In June, there was plenty of water and current driving us, interspersed by frequent rapids that made us pay attention but were great fun. The most extreme rapids are Lava Falls, considered the fastest navigable falls in the country. Rapids dropped six to ten feet, so we were lower geologically in the layers of rock. It is a mile down from the rim to the river, with colored bands delineating layers of the millions of years the canyon has been wearing away. Our guide knew the geology of the canyon, which was amazing to see before us as we floated along. We stopped overnight on sandbars or sandy shore, and our guides made gourmet dinners on camp stoves. We could have used tents, but the nights were so balmy, we liked to put our bedrolls out under the stars. Except for one morning, one of the women came to breakfast with a dead scorpion she had found on her blanket and killed, keeping it in her pocket! I would not have been so sanguine about it. I would have been quick to brush it off and have no more to do with it.

One day, we came upon a family group onshore with their raft turned over and all their supplies floating down the river. They were not able to turn it over, so four or five women came to their rescue to help turn it back. As we continued down the river, we found their cooler and other gear, so we scooped it up and left it on the shore close to where we found it for them to reclaim. We had no such trouble, even as we got drenched in the whitewater. It was one hundred degrees during the day with hot sun, so we were happy to have the cold water pour over us. We took a side trip to a small stream coming from the cliffside with a waterfall, which was cool to stand under and slide down the smooth rocks to the river.

An added adventure was a helicopter ride out of the canyon up to the rim. I had never been in a helicopter before then, and it was a spectacular view looking back down into the depths of the Grand Canyon. I determined then that I would seek an opportunity to ride in a helicopter again.

* * *

When my husband had a sabbatical from the University of Montana in Missoula, my sister and family came to visit, and we did a whitewater rafting trip on the Clark Fork River. The water was very high after heavy snow had melted in the spring, so the river was fast and rough. The guide had those of us in front leaning over the bow of the raft as we hit rapids to anchor it from being flipped, and of course, we repeatedly got soaked. He asked if the others wanted to trade places, and my sister, brother-in-law, and niece said, "No, thanks." So the guide turned the raft around, stern first, and—like it or not—they too got soaked. All in good fun on a warm day.

I was with a group of women whitewater rafting on the Snake River, starting in Idaho and continuing into Wyoming. We all were wearing life jackets, except one woman who didn't want to mess up her tan. She was sitting on the inflated tube on the side when we hit a rock, and she bounced off into the icy rapids. I was on the same side and handed her my paddle to grab onto until we could get her back in the raft. The guide asked me how I knew to do that, but it was automatic for me, with my Water Safety Instructor training many years before. The first thing you try to do with a person who needs help in the water is a reaching assist. Then, cold as she was, a couple of us gave her our dry and warm life jackets and a towel or two. Suntan be damned!

I have also rafted in whitewater in Alaska. Talk about cold! And in the rain forest in Costa Rica—nice and warm with a great view of the birds in the jungle. Cold or warm, we always wear life jackets. Water and adventure...what's not to like?

EXPEDITION SHIPS

Some of my most exciting experiences on the water were on expedition ships to amazing places. The first was around the southern tip of South America to "round the Horn" from the calm south Atlantic Ocean to the typically rough South Pacific, one of the most difficult places in the world to sail. The storms are bigger, the winds stronger, and the seas rougher than anywhere else on earth. After gathering in Buenos Aires, we were able to explore parts of Patagonia before flying to the city of Ushuaia, Argentina, the southernmost city in the world, called "the end of the world."

Our excursion was on a small but rugged ship that held about one hundred passengers. We motored down the Strait of Magellan through the islands of Tierra del Fuego, learning about the history of that name—land of fire. The original missionaries who explored this area in the 16th century found the natives mostly naked but keeping warm with fires in the bottom of their wooden canoes. From a distance, explorers saw lots of fires. While I was experiencing this route, I was reading a contemporary book called *Rounding the Horn* by Dallas Murphy. Two men sailed a small boat in the same passage to repeat the route that Magellan and other explorers had taken hundreds of years ago. For once, I was glad to be on a substantial expedition ship instead of my forty-foot sailboat!

On the calm, east side of the cape, we anchored and climbed the rocks to the marker indicating the southernmost point of South America. It was March, summer in the southern hemisphere, but we climbed in a sleet storm. We took the obligatory photos in the wind, proving we had been there, but happy to climb back down to the boat.

The captain had an open bridge, which meant passengers were welcome to go up to where he was steering the ship. I, of course, took advantage of the offer. I asked about seeing the Southern Cross constellation, which was only visible in the dark sky after midnight, so I was on the bridge to see it at night. That is another iconic wish of sailors.

The captain had suggested to the passengers that maybe we should go back west through the Strait of Magellan instead of rounding Cape Horn because the seas were so rough on the west side. There were several sailor passengers, including me, who objected, saying the reason we were on this voyage was to experience sailing around Cape Horn. So we proceeded to do so. I was on the bridge when we went across the longitude theoretically marking the division between the Atlantic and Pacific Oceans, and immediately, we hit the wild, rough seas with winds from the west the whole stretch of the South Pacific, just as he had predicted. I was fascinated but stayed there too long and didn't take my seasick pills in time, so when I went below, I immediately got sick. But it was worth it.

After a few hours, the seas calmed down, and we were able to go off course to visit Diego Ramirez Island, which is a rookery for albatross. It is not on the typical route for ships in the far South Pacific, so it was a special experience to go there. The hillside was covered with nests of white fluffy albatross chicks. We walked carefully so as not to disturb them, but of course, they never see humans, so they weren't bothered by us at all. We continued our cruise up the west coast of South America to Chile and got to hike into Torres del Paine, a spectacular national park in the Andes with one of the few glaciers in the world that is not shrinking from global warming. Our voyage ended in Santiago, Chile.

＊＊＊

Another expedition trek that was a great experience was from Ushuaia, Argentina, to Antarctica. Before we left, we had lunch at a restaurant on the mountainside above the harbor. Looking down, we saw a huge cruise ship heading through the relatively calm Strait of Magellan to the west coast of South America, next to our small expedition ship heading across the sometimes-angry Drake Passage to Antarctica. There were ninety passengers from all over the world and a very skilled and knowledgeable international crew. We were in luck to have calm seas for the crossing of the Drake. It is notorious for rough seas, just as Cape Horn is. It took a day and a night to cross, so while cold, we could be on the deck to watch the petrels and albatrosses that followed the ship. I am not superstitious, but I knew about the myth of the albatross being a harbinger of doom. The captain opened the bridge, so I went up to follow the navigation and see the view as we approached land.

Our first landing was to be at Cape Wild on Elephant Island, the place that Shackleton's crew spent the winter after their ship *Endurance* was frozen into the ice and broke up. However, after a calm sea crossing, the winds were strong and waves too powerful for us to disembark at the island. It was just as well because it is a rocky, barren spit of land with sea on both sides that are not at all welcoming. It is incredible that Shackleton's crew was able to survive there until rescued months later. We were happy to look from the ship instead of setting foot on land. From there, we proceeded down the east coast of the Antarctic Peninsula and experienced strong winds. We did have several places where we could disembark. We had to bring boots that came up to or over our knees because getting out of the Zodiacs onshore was often windy and wet. We were able to hike on the glaciers and snowfields.

My favorite part of the trip was spent in the Zodiacs exploring Antarctic Sound, called "Iceberg Alley." The huge floating icebergs consist of all shapes and colors that are a photographer's dream. We watched huge chunks calve, breaking off the snowfield into the ocean. Some of the bergs are so huge that they float for years.

We didn't go as far south as the Antarctic Circle (that would have taken another day's sail), but we explored the west coast. We sailed into Deception Island, so-called because you can't see the opening to the bay from the outside. But once in the protected bay, you can see the remains of a fishing camp from the days when whalers were sailing the area. There was a hot spring near shore, so our captain challenged passengers to put swimsuits on under our coats and gear and get in. It was January, summer there, but the air was about forty degrees. When our friends at home asked if it wasn't too cold to go to Antarctica, we pointed out that it was thirty degrees warmer than Chicago in January! The challenge was to strip down, run into the icy water first, then go back to sit in the hot spring to thaw out. My friend Richard took the challenge with a lot of others, but I didn't like the idea of having a wet bathing suit under my clothes when I got out, so I was chicken.

Each time we got back on the ship after our excursions, we were greeted with warm drinks and had gourmet meals and expert guides—a geologist, a historian, a bird naturalist, and a photographer. Richard had not been especially eager to go on this trip but did so because it was at the top of my life list. However, afterward, he said it was the best trip he had ever taken, and he was a world traveler too. Going to Antarctica was my seventh continent. I had experienced them all.

A longtime goal was to visit the Galápagos Islands off the coast of Ecuador. Again, with my friend Wendy, we flew from Guayaquil, Ecuador, to Baltra Island, where we got on the boat that held about eighty passengers plus crew. The waters around the islands are typically calm, being in an area of the Pacific that never gets cyclones or other storms. We took shore excursions each day and sailed between islands to anchor at a different island each evening. One highlight in the water was the opportunity to swim and snorkel off the beach of Bartolomé Island around to the south side of a point to swim with Galápagos penguins. These penguins live farther north than any others in the world. They were driven there by the Antarctic currents that move up the west coast of South America just as far as the Galápagos Islands. I wish I had brought an underwater camera, as I just have a mental picture of Wendy treading water, looking at a penguin face-to-face. They are little friendly-looking birds that act as if they are not at all intimidated by people. We also swam with sea turtles below us and found we could not keep up with them. As big and bulky as they are, they move fast in the water. Galápagos is an amazing experience. Read more about my experiences with the animals there in the "Nature" chapter.

LIVE-ABOARD SMALL BOATS

Some of the best and worst boating experiences I've had have been on small boats that I called home for several days. One of the best was on a *gulet*, a traditional Turkish motor/sailor along the Turquoise Coast of the Mediterranean. Did you know that *turquoise* is the French word for Turkish? The coast water is truly turquoise-clear and shimmering blue-green. The gulets hold six to eight passengers plus the crew: a captain, first mate, and a chef. We sailed when the wind was right and motored when necessary. The gulet had a nice stern deck to relax in the sun or shade and small cabins with portholes for air. We could help sail the boat if we wished (which I always wanted to do) or relax and let the crew do the work.

We stopped at all the cities from antiquity along the coast. For me, it was the best of two worlds—on the sea *and* exploring ancient ruins. We left the boat at one point to hike across the low mountains, with the boat ready to pick us up at the end of the hike. Hot and tired, we put on our suits and swam in what was Cleopatra's Baths, which are said to have been a gift from Mark Antony to her more than two thousand years ago. They are rocks with deep indentations that hold warm seawater. More about the ruins we visited in chapter 6, "Architecture, Archeology, and Artifacts."

* * *

The worst experience on a small boat was in the Greek isles. The year my husband died, we had reserved a forty-five-foot sailboat with three other couples to sail in the Ionian Sea in September, the month he died. While grieving, I also longed to do that sail that we had planned. Several years later, I had the opportunity to sail a similar itinerary but on a commercial boat. The trip was advertised as a sailing trip but turned out to be a frustrating experience. We went in September, a bit cooler than the summer, but the boat was a huge disappointment. It was a renovated cargo ship with the hold converted to cabins with portholes that didn't open, and the cabins had no air-conditioning. It had a smelly diesel engine and no mainsail because the galley and dining area had been built where the mast would have held the sail. The jib (foresail) was a baggy old piece of canvas that could hardly be trimmed to hold wind. When I implored the captain to sail, saying we came on the trip because it was advertised as a sailing trip, he would hoist the jib to prove that we couldn't make headway without the engine. The cabins were so hot at night that several of the twelve passengers would take their bedding up to the deck to be able to sleep. Some nights when we were in a port, some of the women would go to shore and rent hotel rooms to be able to get a good night's sleep.

That negative experience unfortunately influenced the whole trip. We visited some less touristy islands and had great local guides, but the accommodations detracted from the rest of the trip. I don't even remember if we had decent food or not. One aspect of the trip, however, was super. I had not been to Greece before, and having the opportunity to visit the Acropolis and archeology museum in Athens was a memorable experience. In Athens, we had dinner at a rooftop restaurant with a view of the lights on the Acropolis that was magical. The whole trip was not a loss, but what a shame to be miserable on the boat when visiting such an interesting part of the world.

A barge trip in France had been on my wish list for years. Finally, in 2018, I was able to arrange a trip for ten friends on the barge Deborah on the Loire Canal. The canal was built in the 19th century because the Loire River is too shallow in parts for commercial travel. There are dozens of locks on the section we traveled from Nevers to Briare in Burgundy, as the land slopes on the way from the inland toward the coast. Our intent was to travel on the barge but also have the opportunity to bike along on the towpaths some days. The barge had bikes, but we were never in the right location when we stopped overnight to be able to get to the path for bikes. That was disappointing, but the rest of the trip was superb.

We had interesting excursions each day with local guides: a 12th-century monastery being renovated, a medieval town and church, and a vineyard tour and wine tasting, where we learned that the soil is what determines the sweetness of the wines. They were all Pouilly-Fumé, but different soils cause sweeter, dryer (*sec*), or fruity wines. I knew that *fumé* in French meant "smoked," but I didn't know why the wine was called that. I learned that the bloom on the grapes causes a dusty haze when picked, so it got the name *fumé*.

There were seventeen passengers, including our ten Americans. The other seven passengers were French, so it was fun for me to speak French with them, especially with a lady who offered a reciprocal. She would practice her English with me, and I would practice my French with her. A unique experience on the Loire Canal is the aqueduct that the barge navigates to cross over the Loire River. I had never been on a boat bridge crossing over another body of water underneath. One other American on the trip was a crusty old travel writer who had written books about barge trips. He rated our trip mediocre, but the rest of us thought it was great, with gourmet French food, French wines with lunch and dinner, and a very attentive crew. We had a cheese course during each lunch, which featured two cheeses from different regions of France. The barge was newly built for passengers, not a refitted cargo vessel, and it even had a hot tub/spa on deck. We enjoyed sitting in the pool with a glass of champagne, looking at the night sky. One of my friends described the trip as "floating through an Impressionist painting!" *C'était merveilleux!*

On a trip to Vietnam, we took a junk out from Hanoi into Hạ Long Bay, a World Heritage Site. A highlight of the trip was the hundreds of limestone karsts that we sailed among. The boat was old and wooden but well maintained, and we ate freshly caught shrimp and fish each night for dinner. I usually don't have trouble eating local food on all my travels, but one of those meals caused me to get sick. Luckily, the water was smooth, so there was no seasickness to complicate my recovery, and I did enjoy being in the South China Sea.

Also, while in Vietnam, we traveled down the Mekong River from Ho Chi Minh City (formerly Saigon) to Can Tho in a small launch. Along the way, we stopped to give gifts to a family the boat driver helped support, and then we stopped at a pleasant restaurant onshore. We arrived at the floating markets, where all the vendors were selling produce from their flatboats on floating mats spread out in front of them on the water. They live by the river, grow or catch their wares, and make their living from people like us who visit on boats.

I have taken several trips on riverboats. We took a delightful one down the Amstel River, starting in Amsterdam and traveling through the Netherlands and Belgium on the Rhine

Canal. My friend Wendy and I went a couple of days early to explore the Keukenhof Gardens, which are a massive work of art with thousands of tulips that bloom in April. We also spent time in the Rijksmuseum with all the Dutch masters' exhibits. Wendy commented about how refreshing it was to see paintings of daily life and citizens from the Renaissance period instead of all the religious paintings of Italy, and I was thinking the same thing. From Amsterdam, we traveled the canals and passed fields of tulips in bloom. We cruised to Rotterdam and the coast, where we saw the Delta Project, which is an engineering feat of barrier gates instead of dams to stop floods. The Dutch engineers have developed the technology that the rest of the world's oceanfront cities will need as oceans continue to rise. The trip continued to Bruges, a lovely medieval city in Belgium. I have friends who mostly travel on river trips because it is a relaxing way to travel—not in huge groups, not packing up and moving every couple of days, but seeing lots of sites along the way.

Traveling through Central Europe with Richard, we visited Prague and the Czech Republic, and then we ventured on to Vienna and Bratislava by train (see chapter 5, "Trains, Bikes, and Automobiles"). From Bratislava, Slovakia, we took a riverboat on the Danube to Budapest, Hungary. It is a calm voyage through beautiful, wooded countryside. It is always amazing that heavily populated Europe still has its beautiful countryside, such as the inspiration for "The Blue Danube" waltz. Budapest presents a stunning view of government buildings to visitors arriving by boat on the river. We had a wonderful welcome from my son as we arrived in Budapest. He was living in Bulgaria at the time and had driven north to see us. We were also treated to dinner by a friend from Chicago who had grown up in Hungary and was visiting Budapest at the same time. It is always special while in a new country to be hosted by a local or someone who is native to the country.

* * *

While in Egypt, our main mode of travel was by riverboat on the Nile and Lake Nasser. We flew from Cairo to the Aswan High Dam and boarded our boat to spend several days cruising south to Abu Simbel. We had an excellent guide, who described the ruins we saw along the way and the ancient temples that had been moved when the Aswan Dam was being built, which flooded the whole Nile Valley. It took an international consortium to fund the dismantling of the temples, stone by stone, and to rebuild them on higher ground to save them. They really are ancient treasures, so it was genius to move them instead of letting them be inundated under the new lake. (More on that in chapter 6, "Architecture, Archeology, and Artifacts.") On the way back, we bussed to Aswan to get on our next boat to cruise down the Nile back to Cairo. Driving through the desert, there are no truck stops or gas stations, but in spite of bus problems, we did reach the Nile boat in time and had a lovely cruise for another three days. It's amazing to see the difference between the lush green growth irrigated by the Nile and the absolute dry Sahara Desert a few miles away. It is very obvious why the Egyptian civilization grew and thrived along the Nile and the Delta, but not in most of the rest of the big country.

LOCAL TOUR BOATS

I try to include a local boat excursion on every trip that is not primarily a boat trip. In most cases, they are spectacular experiences—an opportunity to explore major tourist attractions in a way most people couldn't see by other means. For example, the best way to see the famous Norwegian fjords is by an excursion boat that takes passengers deep into the fjords. The water tends to be calm, protected by the huge cliffs on the sides of a fairly narrow but deep inlet. One amazing experience was in the Geiranger Fjord, which is a UNESCO World Heritage Site. It is ten miles long, nine hundred feet deep, with 6,000-foot rock walls, splashing with famous waterfalls. The whole Norwegian west coast of fjords is jaw-dropping awesome, with wooded hillsides, abundant waterfalls, quaint villages nestled in the valleys, and very little other boat traffic.

* * *

I took another excursion in a fjord on the other side of the world—Milford Sound in New Zealand—which is also beautiful. Instead of starting from the ocean and going deep into the fjord as in Norway, here, we started at the inland end and cruised out toward the ocean, stopping just short of the open sea. It got windier the farther out we went. There were cliffs, waterfalls, and seabirds that followed along.

On the North Island in New Zealand, we were able to go out in a Māori war boat, which is a thirty-foot wood-carved boat that held the six in my group, plus a few other tourists. We all had paddles and were instructed by the leader on the Māori by his commands that got us all paddling together and hooting war chants to scare away the enemy. It was chilly, and we all wore jackets, but our indigenous leader was shirtless with war paint on his bare upper body. He was well-padded and accustomed to the weather.

A historical boat ride was on the Bosporus from Istanbul, Turkey, to the Mediterranean Sea. It, too, was narrated as we passed Gallipoli, where an enormously deadly battle of World War I occurred. The Bosporus is a strait, dividing Europe from Asia, and the peninsula was a critical stronghold to protect access to the Black Sea. ANZAC troops (Australia and New Zealand Army Corps), British troops, and US troops fought for the Allies against Ottoman Turks, who were trying to hold the land. Almost half a million men died in that battle, many of whom are buried in the ANZAC cemetery there. Recently, a group of people from New Zealand came to renovate the cemetery and ensure that their countrymen are remembered. Visiting these memorials impresses one with both the sacrifices these young men made as well as the futility of war and battles like these.

* * *

We had a happy experience on a small boat off the coast of Kauai to look for whales. The humpbacks were migrating in February, so we were able to sit offshore and watch them swim by and breach around us. It was a special treat to see a mother and baby. As often as I have seen whales, it is always a thrill to see such huge mammals fairly up close.

* * *

A little launch took us from the shores of Tobago to uninhabited Little Tobago on a birding tour. The waves were strong, so it was a challenge to tie up to a small dock with waves crashing over it and balance on the gunnel as we bobbed while trying to step off. Once safely ashore, we hiked up the wooded hillside to an overlook on the Atlantic Ocean, where we were rewarded with a great view of the open Atlantic and cliffs with flocks of nesting and soaring tropicbirds, large white seabirds with red beaks nesting in the rocky cliffs.

* * *

Recently, I had the opportunity to take a tour on Lake Tahoe, California, to Emerald Bay. This was in March while on a ski trip to Heavenly Valley ski area. It was a sunset cruise, though it was a cloudy day. We were served champagne and hors d'oeuvres, and the skipper narrated the history of the beautiful secluded bay that had been privately owned until it became a state park. It's always fun to see the sights from a different perspective than from land.

FERRIES

Trips on ferry boats to get from here to there seem rather mundane, but I have had some interesting experiences on ferries. The first time Bill and I went to Europe, we took a ferry from Dover, England, across the English Channel to Le Havre, France. It was a very rough crossing and was, in fact, the last boat they allowed to cross that day because of the weather. The aspect I remember most was that virtually everyone on board was seasick. I couldn't go into the bathroom because it was so smelly and full of women being sick. I found a spot near the railing outside on the deck and stood there looking ahead with the cold wind blowing in my face. I felt woozy but didn't get sick. Bill wasn't so lucky. For a sailor, he always had a problem with seasickness. We were encouraged to eat, but the idea of food didn't appeal at all. It was my first experience on the ocean and not a positive one!

A more pleasant ferry ride was from Copenhagen, Denmark, to Oslo, Norway, across the Skagerrak, a branch of the North Sea. It was calmer than the English Channel, at least that day, and we had a nice buffet on board. There was a huge pile of shrimp that a group of Asians rushed to and scooped up. I didn't know if that was a delicacy for them or if they were glad to see some familiar food. There was lots of other food for the rest of the passengers, though. I had been to Denmark before but not Norway, so coming into the harbor was a beautiful way to be introduced to a new country for me. Oslo is on the lee side of the country in a deep harbor, protected from the North Atlantic, which has carved the fjords into the west coast.

* * *

I have taken many ferries in the US, especially living near the Great Lakes. There is a ferry that goes from the northern tip of Michigan on the Upper Peninsula to Isle Royale National Park, a two-hour ride across to the Northern edge of Lake Superior. That can be very stormy, but the times I have crossed have been calm. No cars are allowed on the island, so we hired a caddy to carry our gear to a nearby cottage and spent the week exploring on foot. These boats are enclosed so people can sit inside or be out on the deck with cold spray in their faces. Many years ago, we took a boat from Superior, Wisconsin, out to the Madeline Islands in Lake Superior. That, too, can be a rough trip, but we managed to do it on a decent day and camped on the island for a couple of days before returning.

There is a ferry that goes across Lake Michigan from Milwaukee, Wisconsin, to Muskegon, Michigan. Again, one takes a chance on a smooth or rough ride, but it cuts the distance significantly and saves driving through Chicago traffic around the south end of Lake Michigan. There is a ferry that goes from the tip of Door County, Wisconsin, to Washington Island across Death's Door, a strait that has currents and winds and holds many shipwrecks. Luckily, when I first took the ferry across, the only casualty was a pie I had baked for our hosts, who had a cabin on Washington Island. Pies don't travel well on rough boat rides!

CRUISE SHIPS

As you have been reading, I am not a cruise ship fan. I did go on one cruise because friends were going and invited Richard and me to join them, and I liked the itinerary. We started in Montreal, stopped at Quebec City, and cruised the Saint Lawrence Seaway past the Gaspé Peninsula, along Canada's Maritime provinces and the coast of New England, and landed in Boston for the fourth of July.

The ship was not as large as some, holding *only* about 1,500 passengers. That is about 1,400 too many for me. It was, as I understand it, a typical cruise ship with lots of restaurants, an art gallery with paintings on velvet, vendors selling jewelry, and deck chairs, though it was too cold for sunning.

There were some interesting shore visits, such as a walk with a local history scholar in Charlottetown, Prince Edward Island, and a sail on a tall schooner on the Bras d'Or Lake in Nova Scotia. We were able to kayak in a calm area of the Nova Scotia coast and enjoy a drive on Mount Desert Island, Maine, to see the summer homes of the wealthy residents. As they say, the cheaper it is to get on a cruise, the more expensive it is to get off.

My great disappointment, though, was that we went by the Gaspé Peninsula at night, one of the places I had always wanted to see and a key reason I went on the trip. The Gaspé is a spectacular cliff that can only be seen from the river.

We did enjoy a good lobster bake and a visit to Arcadia National Park, Maine, and got to Boston to hear the symphony play the *1812 Overture*. Unfortunately, it was a stormy night, so we listened to the music on TV in our hotel room!

SAILING THE SEVEN SEAS

To the ancient Greeks, the seven seas were the Aegean, Adriatic, Mediterranean, Black, Red, Caspian, and the Persian Gulf.

To medieval Europe, the seven seas were the North Sea, Baltic, Atlantic, Mediterranean, Black, Red, and Arabian.

After Europeans "discovered" North America, the seven seas were the Arctic, Atlantic, Indian, Pacific, Mediterranean, Caribbean, and the Gulf of Mexico.

Today, the iconic seven seas are considered the Arctic, North Atlantic, South Atlantic, North Pacific, South Pacific, Antarctic, and Indian.

So whichever list I choose, I have been on a boat on six of them. I have not yet been on the Indian Ocean or the Arabian Sea, which is the northern part of the Indian Ocean. Nor have I yet been on the Caspian Sea or the Persian Gulf, so I am lacking those seas in Asia, but I have been on the South China Sea and the Andaman Sea in Asia. I have sailed the Gulf of California and many other gulfs, bays, and harbors around the world. Still more seas to sail on!

"A ship in the harbor is safe, but that's not what ships are built for."

—WILLIAM SHEDD

Chapter 2

ICE AND SNOW

"The mountains are calling and I must go."

—JOHN MUIR

Growing up in Minnesota, we spent a lot of time outdoors. In the winter, my mother would make us get outside to get vitamin D from the sun when it was shining. Outside, when it was cold and snowy, we couldn't just stand there, we had to do something! So we sledded, skated, and walked across the frozen lake to town. It was about three miles around the lake to town, but only one mile walking across the ice. Sometimes we skated on the lake, but it was often covered in snow, so my dad would shovel a rink for us, but even then, it was often bumpy ice.

SKIING

When I was thirteen, I got my first pair of skis for Christmas, and skiing became my first choice of winter activity. Those skis were long, wooden, and had bear-trap bindings. At first, I just skied on our sledding hill, climbing back up like we did with the sleds. But we quickly found our way to some small ski areas nearby in Wisconsin: Trollhaugen, Telemark, Hardscrabble. A couple of those aren't even there anymore, but they were great for us kids. Unfortunately, I didn't take any lessons for several years and developed every mistake possible.

It wasn't until I got married, when we took our first trip to Colorado to ski in the 1960s, that I finally took a lesson. Bill was a much better skier than I was (he could learn to do anything by reading, and he taught himself to ski by the book!), so I was determined to take a lesson. We got to Aspen and signed up for lessons, but even though we should have been in different levels, they didn't have enough students, which meant putting us both in the same class—just the two of us. The instructor took us to terrain he wanted to ski with Bill, and I tagged along, even though I didn't belong there. But I was taught to tuck one knee behind the other: "Pretend you are holding a twenty-dollar bill between your knees!" which is the opposite from what we do today with "independent leg action."

Anyway, I fell in love with skiing in the mountains. The silence, the glistening snow on the evergreens, the warm winter sun, and sometimes soft powder to ski in. After that introduction, we took trips to Colorado for many years during the first week in April, which was when Bill had his spring vacation. A few years after our first Aspen trip, Vail was opened and became our favorite ski area.

At home, we skied often at Wilmot Mountain, an area in southern Wisconsin built on a terminal moraine. That means it is a long series of hills, but not high. There are lots of short runs with mostly machine-made snow. Bill joined the National Ski Patrol, and I started teaching skiing, eventually becoming fully certified by passing Professional Ski Instructor tests of both skiing and teaching. When our boys were six and four, they started going to Wilmot with us each weekend. They joined the Mighty Mites for fun and met other kids. They all received lessons that, years later, made them excellent skiers. Mike, the younger, more competitive one, started ski racing at nine and continued through high school at Wilmot. He even chose a college in the West where he could race with the ski team. Steen, our older son, joined the Junior Ski Patrol in high school and went west to college in Montana, where he continued to ski and patrol.

* * *

We continued to ski at Vail over the years, staying with a good friend who had started with the Professional Ski Patrol and moved up to Patrol Director and, eventually, Vice President of Mountain Operations. We were always welcome to stay at his house, and we got to know many locals. We would drive from Illinois overnight, put our skis on at 9 a.m., and go to the top of the mountain at twelve thousand feet with people who lived locally and skied at that altitude all winter. I fought altitude sickness until a friend who is a physiologist explained the cause, which is an imbalance of oxygen and carbon dioxide. I found that taking diuretics for a few days before the trip reduced the reaction to the altitude. There was no way I was going to miss a day of skiing while I acclimatized. I finally learned that it was better to fly out, spend a day acclimatizing, and start skiing the next day.

Spring skiing meant we sometimes had winter snow, sometimes spring corn snow, occasionally powder, but more often slush. I experienced and loved all conditions, most of which we didn't experience in the Midwest. I followed friends around the mountain, skiing every run at this huge area at one time or another. Sometimes I barely kept up but learned to ski much faster than there was room to in the Midwest. I was never injured at Vail, but I did break a leg at Wilmot after skiing through a puddle in a January thaw. My boot froze to my ski, so when I fell and twisted in some crud (gooey deep snow), my leg bones gave way instead of my bindings. This was in 1969, and since then, ski bindings (and skis) have improved significantly, and that kind of accident doesn't happen today.

We occasionally skied at other areas. An especially memorable trip happened one Christmas when both sons were in college in the West. Instead of having them come home, we took Christmas to Big Sky, Montana. Steen cut a tree down in the woods in Montana, and we trimmed it with old-fashioned decorations and had Christmas dinner at the Huntley Lodge. We skied each day, except one when we drove to Yellowstone National Park and rented snowmobiles. We had a ball driving on the snow-packed roads of the park to Old Faithful and sat on the stone wall, watching the geyser blow on schedule. It was bitterly cold but sunny, and we were dressed in warm ski gear. The kids still talk about that week decades later.

I had another chance to explore Yellowstone in the winter when I recently skied at Big Sky again. We took a day off to ride a snow coach through the park, stopping to watch the herds of bison grazing and seeing glimpses of other wildlife. The park is spectacularly beautiful in winter with frozen waterfalls, expanses of snowy mountainsides, and few tourists.

Whitefish Mountain in Northern Montana is known for its fog. The first day we skied there, it was so foggy you could barely see the skier in front of you. We got off the lift at the top, and as I was following the rope that marks the edge of the ski area, I said, "I hope no one is following me because I don't know where I am going." Then I turned around, and everyone who was getting off the lift was indeed in a line behind me! Skiing there again a few years ago, we had pea-soup fog. This time, we were skiing with a mountain guide, so we had confidence *he* knew where he was going. They are so used to the fog that he said this fog didn't even count because we could see him a few feet ahead of us. But the next day, when we were on our own, and the fog had cleared, we realized we had skied down a narrow ridge with drop-offs on either side. Good thing we had been obediently following the Pied Piper!

The Simonsens skied in the winter and sailed in the summer.

After Bill died and I retired, I was determined to keep skiing. Our friends at Vail had retired or moved away, and a friend invited me to join her in a local ski club for people over fifty. It turned out to be a good move since many members were also widows or had a spouse who didn't ski anymore, which meant most of us were solo, looking for ski buddies. We took a couple of trips to the West each year, which introduced me to many ski areas I had not skied before.

One friend I ski with is the most observant—she notices the wind whistling through the evergreen treetops, a small mammal scurrying across the snow, the sun glinting on the clouds. Sometimes she will stop and say, "Look at the view!" By contrast, the guys I ski with are mostly skiing as fast as they can, and that is exhilarating too.

I am happy in any area and at any speed as long as the snow is good. I only complain when it is icy! (Which is why I don't like to ski in New England.) Years ago, we had a friend who had gone to Dartmouth College in New Hampshire and skied the New England narrow trails with typically icy conditions. He perfected his checking skills, setting edges so hard they could chip a bit of ice out from under the skis. Skiing with him in Colorado on a bump run, he lost his path, shot into the woods, checked against a rolled-up snow fence, and bounced back onto the run without missing a beat. His hit caused the snow fence to unroll itself down the mountainside after him! I wish we had cell phones back then to take a spontaneous video!

* * *

My granddaughter grew up skiing at Squaw Valley, at Lake Tahoe, California, starting at age three. She was happy skiing between her Daddy's legs but not happy to be left with an instructor/babysitter for a lesson. But fourteen years later, she is a superb skier, even faster than her grandma now, but she waits patiently for me at the lifts. I told her that in sixty-five years, she will ski slower too!

We have great family ski vacations in the West.

* * *

Over the years, I have skied in Europe several times. In
Northern Italy in the Dolomites, we experienced the most
variety of lifts. From town, we took a gondola up the mountain, and of course, there were chairlifts but also a funicular
cog railway up one mountain, T-bars, and a "magic carpet"
often used for little kids learning, but this was the way

up a small hill. We also had a T-bar tow in a clearing in a farm field, where the farmers get paid in the winter for the number of skiers on their property. The most unique tow I have ever experienced was a team of horses pulling heavy hawser ropes with knots that we grabbed hold of and were pulled along across a flat to the next uphill lift.

Ski etiquette varies in countries. German and Italian skiers are particularly aggressive, pushing past people in front of them in the line and stomping on others' skis. In Italy, I had to learn to use my elbows and ski poles to keep from being pushed into the pit while thirty people tried to fit into a gondola that holds eight. There was a lift operator leaning against the wall watching the chaos of people trying to load the gondola. I said to my friend, if this was Vail, that guy would be counting eight people for each car, and he said emphatically, "Peggy, this isn't Vail!"

Once, while skiing in Morzine, France, it was amazing that the ski area was open at all; the snow was so poor. (We had made our reservations the previous summer when the snow conditions were not yet known.) To get to the mountain inn for lunch, we had a choice of a run that was brown with mud or one that looked better, but we discovered that it was full of rocks. Leaving the inn with a crowd of people, we were like ants swarming down a narrow run with mushed up snow. To make matters worse, we had to take a bus from the mountain base to our hotel. We got on a particularly crowded bus and needed to get off at the first stop. I was standing at the top of the stairs in the back of the bus holding my skis and poles, and tried to step down at our stop. A German man was standing on the bottom step and refused to move so I could get off. People were yelling at him in all languages and telling the driver not to drive on, but he stood there. When I tried to push past him, he socked me in the stomach. Finally, the crowd made him step off and back on so I could get off the bus.

In the US, most skiers are more patient and considerate of others, lining up in mazes to get onto a lift, knowing to alternate as lines merge. But one time at Vail with our friend who was in charge of the mountain, he was standing in the lift line with us when a couple skied up to the ski school entrance. Brian scooted over to them and politely told them that this line was not for the public, but they said something to him in German and got on the chairlift anyway. So he got on his radio and contacted the patrol at the top of the lift, who was waiting for that couple and took their lift tickets away. We laughed that they had defied the wrong person!

A particularly large area in the French Alps is actually three mountains, and their towns are connected by runs and lifts. Trois Vallées includes Courchevel, Méribel, and Val Thorens, with thousands of skiable acres.

Once, when skiing quite fast, probably about forty-five miles per hour on a wide-open slope, I skied over a rise and turned quickly to miss a "death cookie"—a frozen lump of ice left by the grooming machine. A woman, whom I didn't know was behind me, didn't turn in time and crashed into me. (The skier behind is *always* responsible for avoiding the one in front.) We "bought the farm," as they say, with ourselves and our gear spread over the mountainside. Just as in a car, the faster you are going, the harder you crash. As we gathered ourselves together, hurting, we had to ski to the bottom of Courchevel and up a lift and down another mountain to get back to Méribel, where we limped into a clinic. I couldn't use my left arm or ski poles, and my hip hurt where I had landed. After X-rays and seeing an orthopedist, it turned out I had broken my humerus at the shoulder and had a large hematoma on my hip. Mary had a broken rib. Luckily, we were near the end of the trip, and I had a friend who carried my skis at the airport. The X-rays, radiologist, orthopedist, strap to hold my arm to my body, and pain pills in France cost $275. When I got home, I went to an ortho here, who just looked at the X-rays I brought back. He charged $800! So if you are going to break a bone, do it in France!

Another injury happened in the US while skiing at Telluride, Colorado. Again, it was caused by a death cookie. I was skiing fast on a blue (intermediate) run that had been nicely groomed, and I kept going when the run became black-expert. That part of the run had been groomed the day before and had frozen solid with chunks of frozen ice in the snow. I cranked into a turn to slow down, hit the chunk of ice, and flipped, landing on my hip. Again I skied down, took the chair up to catch up with my group, and only then did I realize that I couldn't walk. I skied down to our condo alongside a run, iced, and took a pain pill. I didn't leave the condo for the last day of the trip. We joked that the run had been groomed by a Zamboni, the machine that smooths the ice for hockey and figure skating. There was not a flake of soft snow on it. I used a ski pole as a cane and went to the orthopedist when I got home to find out that I had cracked my sacrum—the flat bone beside the spine. I was mobile, and there was nothing to do for that kind of break but take pain pills, wait, and heal.

Lest it sounds like I am a glutton for punishment, and when people ask me why I keep skiing, I point out that I have skied for sixty-five years, so only three serious injuries is a pretty good record. I don't ski as fast on hard snow anymore, though.

The wonderful mountain air, the glistening snow in the sun, the views from the mountains, the exhilaration of skiing well in various conditions, the sheer joy of floating through powder snow, après ski with friends—all these things make skiing so enjoyable. I tend to forget the few times that have not been so good.

Let me tell you about some of the wonderful places I have skied. The view of the Gore Range from the top of Vail Mountain at 12,500 feet, the top of Zermatt in Switzerland looking across the range at the craggy Matterhorn, and skiing down the back side into Italy.

The glass-bottomed Peak 2 Peak Gondola that crosses the valley between Whistler Mountain and Blackcomb in British Columbia thousands of feet in the air; the view of Lake Louise from the mountain in Banff National Park, Alberta; the sheer expanse of Mammoth Mountain in California; skiing the volcano cone at Mount Bachelor, Oregon; the powder snow in the back bowls of Vail; carving fast turns in soft snow at Snowmass, Colorado; skiing with my son and granddaughter at Squaw Valley, California. These are some of the highs of skiing. Add to that the ambience in Europe of stopping for lunch at the *relais* or *refuges*—mountain inns— with gourmet food and the quaint mountain towns. In the US, the après ski at amazing resorts and then soaking in a spa or hot tub to relax the muscles, maybe with snowflakes falling on our heads. There is a saying in the ski crowd: "Cruise, booze, Jacuzz, and snooze," in that order.

I have skied most of the mountain ranges in North America: the Colorado Rockies, Canadian Rockies, Sierra Nevada, Cascades, Tetons, Wasatch, Sangre de Christo, White Mountains, Appalachians. And in Europe: French and Swiss Alps and the Italian Dolomites, and I don't plan to stop soon!

CROSS-COUNTRY SKIING

I first experienced cross-country skiing (also called Nordic) while we were living in Montana when my husband had a sabbatical leave at the University of Montana. One weekend, we rented gear and took a Saturday to ski from the top of a local mountain to the bottom, where we winter camped. Even though we had never skied on "skinny skis" and were definitely novices, we had such a great time, I determined that when we got back to Illinois, I would buy cross-country skis and go into our woods. We lived next to a forest preserve northwest of Chicago, so when we got snow, I could ski through my neighbor's yard and onto a trail in the woods. It was definitely not the same experience as skiing down a mountain with deep snow in Montana, but I loved going out right after a snowfall for a brief exertion in the woods, sometimes bushwhacking when I got off the trail. When we had our German Shepherd–Husky dog, she loved running alongside me while I skied and then would come home exhausted and happy.

One New Year's Eve, we invited friends for a cross-country ski party with the plan to ski a couple of hours and then come home for a chili supper. The snow was sparse but snowing heavily, so we reversed order and ate first and waited to ski until the snow accumulated a bit more. We had headlamps for everyone and got ourselves to the bike trail in the woods. We celebrated the new year with a bottle of champagne we had carried in a backpack. Friends remembered this unique New Year's Eve for years afterward.

Since I have been retired, I am usually freer to ski the day it snows. Often, the next day, the snow melts or has a wind crust, or dogs and hikers have stomped the ski trail, so it is more fun to go while it is snowing or just when it stops and the sun comes out. I still don't have the skill at cross-country that I do with downhill skiing, but it is exhilarating for a chance to be active outdoors in the winter. I do get to join friends occasionally for a ski outing in the Chicago area, but we don't have many hills, so we usually are trekking on a mostly flat trail. I find my senses are just as alive in the woods here as in the mountains—cold, crisp, sunny, sparkling, white snow on dark branches; silence or occasional crunching; and warmth from the rigorous exercise.

GLACIERS

Antarctica is a continent that has no indigenous population nor government. What it does have is almost entirely covered in ice. What you see of civilization are abandoned whaling stations. Whales were Antarctica's gold rush, and like the end of the gold in California, the whales were decimated.

There are also some historic huts, such as those of Robert Scott, who in 1912 starved to death in his attempt to get to the South Pole and back to the coast. Shackleton's expedition ship *Endurance* was trapped in the ice, and in desperation, the crew had to eat their sled dogs. Some of the crew managed to row for 2,200 miles to South Georgia Island in a small dinghy in the extreme conditions of the Antarctic Ocean to get help to rescue the rest of the crew still stranded on Elephant Island.

The only settlements today in Antarctica are scientific stations that are manned mostly in the summer months (December through about March), though some are working year-round. International treaties declare that scientific exploration and discoveries must be shared internationally, and no country can lay claim to the continent.

A majority of the world's fresh water is trapped in the ice of

Antarctica, but as it melts, it doesn't add to our fresh water supply. The icebergs are so big (some the size of Rhode Island!) that they raise the level of the ocean when they melt. Scientists have put GPS trackers on them to determine where they go and how long they last. As they float north into warmer waters, they melt quickly, adding to the ocean's rise that threatens low-lying island nations, especially in the Indian Ocean and South Pacific.

The whole trip to Antarctica was fascinating. A fun highlight was climbing a glacier and sliding down on our butts—a passel of passengers, many of us well past youth, acting like kids again. The first in line broke trail, and the rest of us went faster down the packed snow. We got up close and personal with colonies of penguins—gentoos, chinstraps, Adélies, and Macaroni, with stringy feathers on their heads.

They are, like the albatross chicks I mentioned earlier, not bothered at all by humans because they have experienced so few of them. We could walk among them and watch their waddling behavior. They eat krill in the ocean, which turns their excrement pink, so there are streams of pink snow where the penguins slide down "penguin highways" to the ocean. The babies had just been born, so we saw both male and female penguins protecting and warming their little furry bodies under their bellies. They ignored us humans as we walked among them. The Weddell seals that lie around on ice floes also barely noticed us.

* * *

I have also hiked on the Mount Cook glacier on the South Island of New Zealand. That's an amazingly diverse environment. The glacier runs down to a rain forest, which grows right down to the ocean. It rains (or snows) so much there that the ranger who guided us up the mountain had a supply of big golf umbrellas to hand out. It was a strange experience hiking up a glacier with umbrellas over our heads in the pouring rain. I have hiked at the base of Mount Rainier in Washington, which is spectacular when "the mountain is out," meaning it is clear of fog or blizzard, and its glaciated peak can be seen. Mountains and snow... what's not to like?

* * *

We first visited Glacier National Park in the 1970s and hiked up to glaciers there too. More recently on a side trip from skiing at Whitefish Mountain, we saw that the glaciers the park is named for are almost all gone. The temperature has warmed enough to melt them in summer, and without constant snow in winter, they are shrinking substantially. Most of the glaciers in the world are melting at unprecedented rates, threatening the water supply for millions of people. India and Pakistan depend on the Himalayan glaciers, which are shrinking. Glaciers in the Andes are receding and increasing the desert areas of South America. You can still see snow at the top of the Andes, but it covers much less mountain area than in the past. For a lover of ice and snow, this is an alarming change in my lifetime.

TUNDRA

After years of wanting to visit Churchill, Manitoba, which is called "the polar bear capital of the world," I finally got to go there to see polar bears up close. We drove over the frozen land in tundra buggies to get to the edge of Hudson Bay. The trucks have huge tires that can grip the ice and snow and put the vehicle high enough to be safe if the bears decide to come close. We were there in November, and the water's edge had frozen early, so most of the bears had already moved out to hunt seals. They go without food for months, and the females nurse their young all summer without much food, so they are hungry when they can get on the ice to catch a seal. We saw many with binoculars, but one lone male came lumbering by our buggy, not paying any attention to us. It was a great photo opportunity, but of course, we were not allowed to get off the vehicle, both for safety and so as not to leave any trace of humans behind. Plants grow so slowly on the tundra with a short growing season and very little soil, so the licensed buggies are the only vehicles allowed in the national park.

We had the opportunity to experience dog sled rides across the tundra in Northern Manitoba. Great fun! I had also been able to drive a sled pulled by a team of dogs in British Columbia. In both environments, the dogs are so anxious to be one of the eight selected to drive a sled and run full speed when allowed to. It was interesting to see the personalities of the dogs and the skill the handlers have to manage them.

* * *

I have also hiked on the tundra in Denali National Park, Alaska. There are no accommodations in the park for the same reasons access is limited at Churchill. Visitors stay at the edge of the park and take hop-on-hop-off buses to get into the park. That way, people can take longer hikes or just stop along the one road to watch animals on the tundra. There are warnings about being in grizzly bear habitat, but also moose, caribou, Dall sheep, and wolves roam there. Of course, I was as interested in the alpine wildflowers as I was the huge mammals. In spite of a short growing season, the long days of summer bring out the best of the wildflowers. In June, when we were there, they were spectacular.

ICE AND SNOW AROUND THE WORLD

I have skied or trekked on glaciers in North and South America, Europe, and New Zealand. I have not been to the Himalayas or other glaciers in Asia and probably won't go, and I certainly will not get to the top of Mount Everest. When I was younger, I experienced altitude sickness at 12,500 feet, so I certainly would not have been able to handle the 29,000 feet of Mount Everest! However, I do appreciate the challenge that attracts those skilled mountain climbers. My draw to snow and ice is as much aesthetic as athletic!

"I wonder if the snow loves the trees and fields, that it kisses them so gently? And then it covers them up snug, you know, with a white quilt; and perhaps it says, 'Go to sleep, darlings, till the summer comes again.'"

—LEWIS CARROLL

Chapter 3

NATURE

"It is in the wild places, in the damp clean air of an ancient forest, on a heaving ocean in unpredictable winds, on a snowy summit on the top of the world that I enter my own personal cathedral and know where I fit in the vastness of creation."

—JIM WHITTAKER

I need to live with trees. I like prairies and coasts and deserts, but I need to live with trees. Growing up, our yard was an acre with lots of trees, and we vacationed every summer camping in the Minnesota Northwoods. My father loved to camp and fish. My mother was a botanist with a PhD in plant ecology. She worked as a researcher at the University of Minnesota. Her love was native wildflowers, so when we camped in the boreal woods, she loved to explore all the little native plants that grew only in that ecology. After she retired, she created mini ecologies in her yard—boreal plants under the pines, deciduous woodland plants under the oaks, a fen with a water-fall and pond, and even a little prairie in one sunny spot. I didn't become a scientist in her footsteps, but I did learn many of the plants by osmosis, and I certainly learned to value the rare wildflowers. But mostly, I learned to love the woods.

Living in Illinois, I have a house with lots of windows on an acre of property and a white oak grove in my backyard, along with the black oaks, shagbark and bitternut hickories, and black walnut trees. (I have a nutty yard!) The Chicago area, I learned, has the greatest plant diversity of any metropolitan area in the country. That is because we are at the southern end of the northern deciduous woodland, at the eastern edge of the tallgrass prairie, and at the northern edge of some warmer climate forbs. In addition, it has the unique climate and plants of the shore of Lake Michigan. In fact, when this area was settled, many of the communities took on the names of their habitat: groves for the wooded areas and parks for the open fields and prairies. So we have many towns with names like Elk Grove, Buffalo Grove, Morton Grove, Deer Grove, and even Lake Forest. The open spaces were named Oak Park, Melrose Park, Schiller Park, Tinley Park, and even Park Forest!

When I retired, I started volunteering with a local conservation organization, Citizens for Conservation, which acquires and restores land to presettlement habitat. While I knew most of the woodland plants from growing up with them, I learned many of the prairie plants from working with experts in restoration. I was able to recognize and protect the remnant native plants in my yard that wanted to live under the oaks and in the wooded area that had not been disturbed when the house was built. I have also planted many more species that thrive in oak woods and a bit of prairie where I have sun. I now have more than two hundred species of native plants in my yard. In addition to traveling to places with forests, I get to live in the woods!

FORESTS

My favorite trees are in the old-growth forests of the Pacific Northwest. I love the redwoods, sequoias, and ponderosas of California and the Douglas firs of Washington. It is as spiritual an experience as a cathedral to walk in the deep shade with rays of sun filtering through towering one-thousand-plus-year-old trees with spongy soil underfoot.

I had never been to Yosemite National Park, and after my husband died in September, that October, my son and daughter-in-law invited me to come out to hike there as a balm for my grief. I remember hiking in the woods, hiding my tears behind my sunglasses, thankful for my son's caring attention, but even sadder that Bill was not there to enjoy it with me. We stayed in platform tents, and Mike and Heather made reservations for dinner at the Ahwahnee Lodge, the iconic hundred-year-old luxury inn, when Heather informed me that she was pregnant with my first grandchild. It was a bittersweet moment that is etched in my mind. I was so happy to know I would have a grandchild but so sad that Bill didn't live to know her.

I have since returned to Yosemite to hike and watch the rock climbers scale Half Dome, and I have visited Sequoia National Park to get my fill of enormous trees. I have also hiked in Redwood National Park, thankful that local environmentalists protected the iconic trees from logging long before the country got around to designating it a national park.

I am lucky to have a sister who has a cabin in the North-woods in Ontario on the shore of the North Channel of Lake Huron. I visit every summer to enjoy the massive cedars and wildflowers, and in the fall, the scarlet maples. My son has a mountain house in Tahoe-Donner near Lake Tahoe on the California-Nevada border. In both cases, we are in the woods—no lawn, just tall evergreens with needle-covered ground and sunlight filtering through the treetops, so it is rarely hot and just warm enough in the summer to be outside all day—and no mosquitoes!

* * *

Years ago, camping in the national forest outside of Yellow-stone National Park, I was in the site alone one evening when Bill and a friend took the car to go fishing. A brown bear came lumbering onto our campsite while I was washing dishes. With only a tent as shelter, I decided to try to scare him away, so I banged some pots that I was washing. I don't know if that actually scared the bear, but he decided I was not worth bothering. He turned and ambled back down the path. Driving through Yellowstone, we would get caught in bear jams, where cars would be blocked by bears on the road and on the cars, sometimes digging into the car top carriers while the owners would sit helplessly inside. Over the years since, and with tourism increasing, rangers have had to move bears into the high country to try to reduce the interaction of bears and people.

We also saw bears in Northern Minnesota. After my father died, my mother was sad that she would not be able to get to the Northwoods anymore, so we three grown kids made a promise that we would take turns planning a family vacation each summer. One year, we rented a houseboat on Rainy Lake at the northern tip of the state. We parked the flat-bottomed boat up against islands each night and explored the woods. It was August, and we wondered why there were no blueberries on the bushes. While exploring in a canoe one night at dusk, we saw why. A mother bear and her cub were on the island eating every berry they could strip from the bushes. We were glad to be offshore in a canoe and not face-to-face with a protective mother bear!

The only time I have seen a grizzly bear nearby was in Alaska's Glacier Bay. We also were able to sit in the kayak safely offshore and watch him rambling along in the lupines onshore, oblivious to us, minding his own business.

One bear we were happy to get up close to was a koala bear in a reserve outside of Sydney, Australia. We were actually able to hold him, a cuddly, furry little creature, but then they don't "koalify" as bears!

On Isle Royale National Park in Lake Superior near the Canadian border, we saw moose grazing. They are amazingly fast runners for such a lumbering animal, so we made a point of staying away, behind some trees so as not to disturb them. They are not aggressive like grizzly bears but could do a lot of damage if they get mad!

We experienced another animal to keep a distance from on the Appalachian Trail in Virginia. I was the advisor to a

Senior Girl Scout troop, and we went on a weeklong backpacking trip on the trail, camping along the way. One night in my backpacking tent with my co-leader, we heard a *lap, lap, lap* in her cup of water by her sleeping bag. We woke up enough to recognize that it was a skunk who had squirmed under the screen on the door and got into our tent. I had visions of burying my tent and bedding and somehow getting myself rid of the smell, but we got lucky. I lay still while my co-leader carefully went to the foot of the bedding, unzipped the screen, and said, "Here, kitty, kitty," and to our relief, the skunk agreed and left the tent without punishing us!

TEMPERATE RAIN FORESTS

Our first trip to the temperate rain forest in Washington state, the Hoh Rain Forest in Olympic National Park, was a spiritual and sensual experience with the dense woods, mossy, moist ground, silence except for the sounds of birds, and the wind softly whispering in the tall trees. That area gets fourteen feet of rain per year! That much rain supports the growth of the huge trees and mosses, but because very little sun gets through the tall tree canopy, understory growth is limited, so you can walk on the moss and look up as if in a cathedral. We hiked the Hall of Mosses trail that lived up to its namesake. I have since also visited temperate rain forests in British Columbia and New Zealand and was happy to return recently to the Hoh again.

* * *

New Zealand's rain forest begins at the base of the Mount Cook Glacier and runs down the mountainside to the ocean. Unfortunately, it was logged in the 20th century, so the trees aren't as huge as those in the Pacific Northwest. It has a jungle feel, though not the same flora as a tropical rain forest. There are rivulets and streams running everywhere, with melting glacial water and rain runoff trickling and pouring down the mountainside. New Zealand's iconic image is the tree fern, a huge prehistoric fern that thrives in the rain forest.

We learned that Australian possums were introduced into New Zealand a century ago for their fur (not the same scrawny opossums we have in the US). Without the predators found in Australia, they have multiplied in New Zealand and are now invasive pests. New Zealand has open hunting season all year to try to control them, but the dense forests that surround the rain forest on the mountainsides make it hard to hunt them. After the possums multiplied, the government introduced stoats, a weasel-like animal that preys on possums and is now itself invasive.

New Zealand is also the country of sheep, one breed of which are merinos, so they make wonderful woven items that are a combination of possum fur and merino wool. The other iconic animal in New Zealand is the kiwi, a flightless bird that lives and lays its eggs on the ground. Historically it was not endangered because there were no predators, but now the stoats go after the kiwi eggs, so the bird has become rare and rarely seen. A proven case of human interference that upsets the natural biodiversity.

JUNGLES AND TROPICAL RAIN FORESTS

A temperate rain forest typically has a very thick canopy of tall trees, which allows very little light to penetrate to the ground level, making it difficult for plants to flourish. A jungle floor, on the other hand, will usually have a thick undergrowth of plants and vegetation. The word *jungle* is Indian, so most forests in Asia and Africa are considered jungles, whereas in Central and South America, they are more likely to be called "rain forests." There is an eerie feeling about jungles so dense that, over the years, they have buried buildings. We saw this in Cambodia, where some medieval temples near Angkor Wat have just been discovered. Because they were so overgrown, no one knew they were there. The same thing happened in Guatemala, where the growth buried pyramids from the 8th and 9th centuries, only to be discovered in the last century.

In Thailand, we rode elephants in the jungle, glad they were sure-footed as they tromped over logs and branches. I had seen elephants up close on a safari in Africa but had never touched one. I was surprised how bristly their hair is. We stayed in treehouse lodging with rooms built up in the trees with a ladder to get to them, keeping the ground critters out, with open walls to the jungle. The bathrooms were the only rooms with half walls. The roof had an overhang, so during the daily rains, the rooms stayed dry. That would not have happened with lodging on the saturated ground. It was amazing, though, that there were no mosquitoes or other bugs. We hiked in a national park with a trail up the mountainside through the woods. But I was nonplussed at some other visitors, like the Japanese ladies hiking in either heels or flip flops!

In the rain forest in Costa Rica, we zip-lined across a huge valley. The beginning of the line went a short distance from one tree to another on the hillside so the less adventurous could bail out and climb down a ladder to the ground. Past that, the zip line was a half-mile long and very high across the mountain valley from one peak to another. I thought it was a blast and a great way to effortlessly zip through the tree canopy.

We also hiked across a rope bridge above a chasm. One has to trust the vines holding the bridge together when you are a thousand feet up! In addition to lots of birds, Costa Rica has sloths, typically fat blobs lying on tree branches. They sleep most of the time, except when they are eating, so it was easy to see where the word *slothful* came from. We also went to a beach on the Atlantic one night with red headlamps so as not to disturb the sea turtles, whose eggs were hatching. The mother turtles were leading the hatchlings from the nests buried in the sand to the sea, where they will live and grow until it is time for them to nest. Then they will return for the first time to this beach.

* * *

In Australia, when I was in Port Douglas for an international conference, we rented a car to drive north into the rain forest. We weren't allowed to take the car on a ford across the river, so we were limited on what we could see. When we found that the river was full of alligators, we were just as happy to see them from the shore. There is a completely different flora in the Australian rain forest, just as so many animals are unique to that continent. I learned about Gondwana, a supercontinent that existed when all the present Southern hemisphere continents, including Australia, were connected 550 million years ago. When Australia separated from Asia (modern-day Malaysia, Vietnam, and the neighboring islands) and Africa about 180 million years ago, compared to the rest of the world, its plants and animals evolved along separate paths, creating unique biodiversity and indigenous flora and fauna.

On a birding trip to Trinidad and Tobago, we hiked through the rain forest with a local guide who could imitate the bird calls so accurately that birds would come, thinking there was another of their species there. The rain forest canopy is so dense that even though I could hear the birds up there, I usually could not see them. Our guide had a scope he would position on a particular bird, and one British couple who were very experienced birders and expert photographers with their huge lenses and bipods would shoot amazing photos of birds I could barely see with my binoculars. At the Asa Wright Nature Centre in the rain forest of Trinidad, we could stand on the balcony and see a huge variety of hummingbirds and others feasting on watermelon at the bird feeders. In a week, we saw 127 species of birds, many of them endemic to either Trinidad or Tobago, like the Trinidad motmots and oilbirds and the Tobago chachalacas. My favorites were the scarlet Ibises we saw in the Caroni Marsh Park. We took a boat ride down the river through mangroves to a lake near the ocean surrounded by rain forest, where flocks of the big red birds came in to roost at dusk. They were in the trees, on the water, and flying overhead. An amazing sight!

On uninhabited Little Tobago, we climbed the wooded hillside to a lookout over the Atlantic Ocean to see the red-billed Tropicbirds nesting in the rocky cliffs. One was right at our feet, sitting on a nest with a fluffy baby, not bothered at all by people walking where it should have been too close for comfort. On the way back, we were able to motor over some coral reefs in the glass-bottomed boat, looking down on the fan and staghorn corals with lots of tropical fish.

In the rain forest on Kauai, Hawaii, we hiked and also flew over in a doors-off helicopter. I loved looking down on the wilderness, especially because we were up there with an unobstructed view. Much of Kauai has vast expanses of banyan trees, an import from Africa that now has overtaken much of the native flora. An innovative approach to getting rid of it has been to build power plants whose fuel is the wood of these trees. The plants in the tropics are very different from those I know in the north, so I have a new challenge to learn them each time I am in a tropical rain forest.

DESERTS

I have visited deserts in North and South America, Africa, the Middle East, and Asia. And visiting is the most I want to do. My brother lives on the Chihuahua Desert in New Mexico, the largest desert in North America. I visit in early spring to see the desert in bloom. It's a fascinating environment, but it's certainly challenging to live there. It is amazing that anything grows there with maybe a couple of inches of rain per year. Hiking in Arches and Canyonlands National Parks in Utah, I learned the need to stay on the path because even a footstep on the fragile soil can kill a plant that took dozens of years to grow less than an inch. I have learned a bit about cactus, their survival adaptations, and the small animals and insects that coexist.

✳ ✳ ✳

The most extreme desert I have experienced is the Sahara, in both Egypt and Morocco. The sheer expanse of sand is incredible. We rode dromedary camels at Giza, where many of the Egyptian pyramids have stood for thousands of years. They are amazingly adapted animals, going days without drinking water, which can be stored in the fat of their humps. My camel was thirsty—his hump was empty and flopped over. Some of the people in our small group were freaked out by being up there on an unpredictable animal, but like the elephants in the jungle, I assumed they were sure-footed, and I just held on when he bent his front legs first, pitching me forward until his back legs were folded so I could get off.

We also went up in hot air balloons at dawn over the Valley of the Queens, a desert valley of dozens of tombs from three to four thousand years ago. They are so well-preserved because the sand covering them protects them from wind erosion. It was a great way to see and take photos of the whole area and gain a perspective on the scope of the burials you don't see when walking around a few of them.

The Sahara in Morocco is beautiful, but it's an amazing expanse of moving dunes. We stayed in upscale tents in the Merzouga area of Morocco. We climbed the dunes to watch the sunset over the horizon and again rode camels across the sands. There is an ancient Berber population of nomads who live on the desert and eke out a life by moving their herds of sheep or goats to find grazing by oases. We visited a Berber widow and her beautiful children under a tarp they use during the day for shade. The area gets a couple of inches of rain per year, so there are a few small streams with just enough plant life for goats to graze on.

In Mongolia, we rode in Russian-made vehicles like Jeeps across the Gobi Desert. There are no roads, so the drivers just drive anywhere, further damaging the fragile environment. We stayed in *gers* (yurts) that are round canvas tents with a frame and floor. Amazingly they each had a solar panel in the front that created enough power for one bare light bulb to hang in the ger. There was a bathroom building with flush toilets and showers. Like any desert, it was hot during the day but cooled off enough at night to sleep. As with so much of the world that has gone from no phones to cell phones, much of Mongolia skipped the infrastructure of an electrical grid and instead went from no electricity to solar power.

In Gobi Gurvansaikhan National Park, we hiked up Eagle Valley, a canyon that has the world's only desert ice cap in the winter, so when it melts, it waters small trees and brush and is cooler. We also climbed the "singing dunes" at Khongoryn Els, so named because the shifting sands make humming sounds if you stand on them and listen. This area is a UNESCO Biosphere Reserve.

We rode camels here in Mongolia, too, the two-humped Bactrian camels. Unlike the camels in Africa, they can withstand the extreme cold of the winters with their thick coat of fur. There are only about one thousand of these camels left in the world. The nomadic herders live on the desert, moving to where there is grazing for the camels. After our ride, we were invited into a herder's ger, and his wife and little daughter offered us camel's milk drinks and a pastry. I was game to try, but I don't like warm milk of any kind and declined when offered a refill!

We were in Mongolia in July to see their annual Naadam Festival, which includes horse races by young children, a wrestling match, and archery. The children start riding horses as toddlers, and at ten or twelve, the best riders enter the Naadam competition, coming into the arena after racing for twenty-five miles! On the steppes, we were able to spot Tahkis, the endangered Mongolian wild horses that are the only truly wild horses still in existence. They have not bred with domestic horses, as have herds elsewhere in the world. Riding horses is a main means of transportation, so of course, we needed to do so too, but not on wild horses!

In Jordan, we rode in 4×4 vehicles across the Red Desert at Wadi Rum. (A wadi is a dry valley with water only in the rainy season). It is a moonscape, bright rust desert sands, with granite and sandstone rock mountains eroded by desert winds.

We saw the Seven Pillars of Wisdom of T. E. Lawrence, who was later called Lawrence of Arabia, though he was actually in Jordan. He cooperated with the Bedouin tribes against the Ottoman Empire. We had lunch at a Bedouin camp, a settlement of these formerly nomadic people. I asked our guide why the country of Jordan is shaped the way it is and not following any natural contours. He said those were the boundaries drawn by the British after World War I and were meant to intentionally divide the territories of the different Bedouin tribes to try to weaken their influence against the British occupiers. Of course, the tribes didn't pay any attention to artificial boundaries in their nomadic movements looking for water and pastures.

Jordan is the driest country in the Middle East, even with the Jordan River. So much water is drawn from the river for irrigation, especially by Israel, that the Dead Sea into which it flows has shrunk by two-thirds in the last seventy years and may dry up like the Aral Sea in Russia if the rate of reduction continues.

PRAIRIES AND SAVANNAS

Illinois is trying to restore a small part of the prairies of the past, for which it was named the Prairie State. Presently, there is less than 1 percent of the original prairies left. One superb restoration is the 3,800-acre Nachusa Grasslands west of Chicago. The site contains numerous prairie remnants, residuals of the most threatened major ecosystem in the world. Volunteers have collaborated with expert staff to restore most of the original native forbs and grasses, and recently, the park has introduced bison herds to recreate the habitat of the prairies that existed here until the early 20th century. The invention of the steel plow by John Deere was a contributor to the breakup of the deep roots of the prairie plants. A group of us nature-lovers visited and had a chance to walk the prairie in bloom but kept a good distance from the bison!

* * *

In addition to the Appalachian Trail hiking trip I took with my Senior Girl Scout troop, we went to the former National Center West in the Wind River Mountains of Wyoming. We drove across South Dakota and the Custer State Park buffalo range. As we were standing outside a fence watching the huge animals, one decided he didn't like us and charged, ramming the fence enough to be able to hit one of the girls and bruise her hip. We learned to keep our distance even when they were fenced in!

* * *

As a volunteer with Citizens for Conservation in the Barrington, Illinois, area, I have learned a lot about prairie plants. In addition to identifying the plants, I now know the conditions they need. There are dry prairie plants, mesic (medium moisture) plants, and those that grow in wet areas of the prairie. We have successfully restored prairies with hundreds of acres of local ecotype prairie plants, receiving a restoration award from the Illinois Environmental Protection Agency. In doing so, we have created a habitat that has attracted endangered birds like bobolinks and Henslow's Sparrows, birds that live only in open prairies, not backyards. I have incorporated a few species of native plants in the small prairie I have planted in a sunny spot in my yard, including those that are magnets for butterflies, bees, and other pollinators.

Citizens for Conservation also received an award for the restoration of a 150-acre savanna, which is the unique combination of oak and hickory open woods on the edge of the prairie. We have a family of sandhill cranes, who come every spring to an island in the wetland on our Flint Creek Savanna to lay their eggs. The island is inviting because it is safe from coyotes. It's fun to see the baby colts hatch and safely grow up before migrating south in the fall.

I saw thousands of sandhill cranes landing in a wetland at Jasper-Pulaski Fish and Wildlife Area in Indiana in the fall as they were migrating south. It was an amazing sight to see them all flocked together, finding a way to land in the midst without landing on top of another crane. We even saw a large bird towering over the sandhills, and on a closer look with binoculars, we realized that it was a whooping crane who tagged along with the sandhills when they passed the crane sanctuary in southern Wisconsin. The whooping cranes are an endangered species being bred at the sanctuary and led by a white-suited driver of a glider to teach them to migrate! Maybe they just need to follow the sandhills.

Internationally, I have had the opportunity to visit savannas in South Africa. The most impressive was Kruger National Park. We went on a safari there to see all the iconic animals that thrive on savannas. The most numerous were the zebras and wildebeests that ran through in hordes. We stayed on the edge of the park in an open-front inn that faced the savanna so we could sit on our balcony to watch the ever-changing panorama. We did have to watch out for monkeys who liked to invade and steal the sugar and creamer coffee supplies in our rooms. We took early morning rides out to find the lions in the bush. Along the way, we saw giraffes and enormous African elephants that came within inches of our vehicles. We, of course, were warned not to put our arms over the edges. The elephants were so huge, they could have knocked our trucks over with a push of their head, but we behaved, and so did they. We also saw dingoes, wild dogs, and hyenas, but no tigers. It is a different experience to see these iconic animals in their natural habitat instead of in zoos.

MOUNTAINS

As you read in chapter 2, most of my experience in the mountains has been skiing. Growing up in the Midwest, there aren't any mountains. Hills, yes, but not mountains. As a small child living in Cheyenne, Wyoming, for six years, we took camping vacations to Rocky Mountain National Park and others nearby. I was eight when we moved back to Minnesota, where I was born, and the camping vacations continued in the woods, sometimes with rocky streams like in the mountains, but no hiking up hills, let alone up mountains.

The first mountain I climbed was Mount Washington in New Hampshire. One summer in college, I taught swimming at a camp in Maine, and we took a side trip to Mount Washington to climb. It is only 6,288 feet high, small by Western standards, but the tallest mountain east of the Mississippi. It was a good challenge for a day's excursion.

My real mountain-climbing challenge came with my husband when we climbed the Tetons in Wyoming with a group of friends. We camped first at Jenny Lake campground at the base of the mountains. Even in the late sixties, the campground was so popular that we had to be there at eight o'clock in the morning, driving around until we saw someone breaking camp so we could quickly claim their spot. We had our backpacking tents and gear, so we were ready to start up the mountain the next day. The base has trails that are steep but manageable. In order to get up to the saddle (ridge) between the peaks, the climb involves scrambling over huge boulders—talus—that is slower going.

We camped each night by a stream and ate freeze-dried food cooked on our little propane Primus stoves. The final day was technical climbing—roped in and climbing the rock face with pitons and carabiners. Since I was pregnant with my first son, I decided not to have a belay rope around my waist with the potential problems that it might cause, so a friend and I waited at the saddle while Bill and his friend Al scaled the cliffs. They didn't reach the summit, though, because a thunderstorm moved in. As we waited, sheltered under a rock overhang, we could see Bill and Al in their orange ponchos bounding over the talus. They were completely exposed to the lightning and needed to get off the rocks as fast as they could. After the storm, we started down, and the next night, we got off the mountain at dusk. We were hungry, tired, and dirty, and really wanted a shower and a good campsite for the night, but there were none to be found, so we pulled into a KOA campground. Since there were no sites available, we convinced the manager to let us pitch our backpacking tents in an open space. During the night, we found out why there were no sites there—we woke up to the smell of sewage. We were camped on a septic field! But before we slept, we all dumped the last of our dried soup into a pot and emptied our canteens into it to make soup. We all chowed down until the bottom of the pot was showing, exposing a few boiled minnows! One guy swore he was going to sue Lipton for contaminated soup, but the reality was that we had filled our canteens in the streams on the mountain and had scooped up the minnows, not to be discovered until we cooked them in the soup pot.

In Montana one summer, when my husband was teaching at a geology field station, I went along with Steen, who was nine months old. On July 29, 1969, I was sitting on the top of a mountain with Steen in the Bridger Wilderness while Bill was fishing. As I looked at the full moon coming up, I said to Steen, "There are men walking around up there." Fifty years later, when NASA was celebrating the Lunar landing of Neil Armstrong and Buzz Aldrin, I reminded Steen of where he was at that momentous moment, and of course, he said he didn't remember it!

Since then, I have hiked other mountains, backpacked in Montana, Utah, and Colorado, and hiked across the top of the pass along US 6 in Colorado, with an altitude at 11,990 feet at Loveland Pass, where it crosses the Continental Divide. In June, the alpine meadow was full of wildflowers. In Montana, when our boys were five and seven, we asked locals to recommend a backpacking trail that was not too difficult for their little legs. We set off on a trail to a campsite that was only a couple of miles from where we parked the car. It was near a lake with good fishing. Each boy had a little backpack to carry his sleeping bag, a change of clothes, and a bottle of water. Our dog had saddlebags to carry her food in and our garbage out, Bill carried the tent, his sleeping bag, and cooking gear, and I carried the food, sleeping bag, and my gear. It all worked beautifully until dusk, when the mosquitoes came out so thick. We built a smoky fire but still had to get into the tent with the smoke coming our way. The fish were jumping for all the mosquitoes, but Bill couldn't stand to be out there fishing. We even had to let the dog into the zipped foyer because she was driven crazy by the mosquitoes too. I had a massive headache from breathing the smoke. We packed out the next morning, and when we asked our friends why they recommended the mosquito hell, they said, "Well, you shouldn't go in June!"

Over the years, I have hiked in several national parks: Denali in Alaska, Glacier in Montana, Crater Lake in Oregon, the Great Smoky Mountains in Kentucky, the Appalachian Trail in Virginia (as I mentioned with my Senior Girl Scout troop),

Isle Royale in Michigan, Arches and Canyonlands in Utah, the Organ Mountains in New Mexico, and Yosemite in California. I have also hiked along the shores of Lake Superior, Lake Michigan, and Lake Tahoe. Yosemite was a test of my continued physical mobility, as the last time I hiked there was six weeks after I had a knee replacement. I didn't push it too hard but found that it worked better and with less pain than it had before the operation. My hiking days continue.

One of the joys of hiking in the mountains is the discovery of mountain lakes and streams. I mentioned Jenny Lake in the Tetons, Crater Lake, and Lake Tahoe (which is the largest alpine lake in North America). In Glacier Park, along Going to the Sun Highway, one comes to beautiful Lake McDonald. It is refreshing after the exertion of a hike up a mountain to rest and perhaps wade a bit in the cold, clear mountain water, which is often snowmelt.

Internationally, I have hiked up mountains in the Swiss Alps, Thailand, Turkey, Wales, New Zealand, and Antarctica. We drove across the Atlas Mountains in Morocco but didn't have time to hike. Those mountains have cedar forests on the west side that get rain but are bare rock on the dry, east sides. We saw a group of Barbary apes in the Middle Atlas Mountains and, of course, herds of sheep and the occasional donkey.

＊ ＊ ＊

We hiked on Table Mountain near Cape Town in South Africa. South Africa is a special place for wildflowers since it is a plant kingdom by itself. Most other plant kingdoms are found in multiple places with similar ecology, such as alpine, which is found in Europe, along with North and South America. Boreal forests are found in Canada, Northern Europe, and Asia. Tropical plant kingdoms are found in South Asia, Africa, and Central and South America. But because South Africa has plants indigenous to mountains, deserts, savannas, forests, and oceanfront, the country itself has been designated a plant kingdom.

* * *

When I arrived at the airport in Auckland, New Zealand, they asked if I had brought hiking boots, and I had, so they confiscated them at customs, took them to sterilize the soles, and brought them back in a plastic bag. The Kiwis are very careful not to allow any alien organisms to be introduced into their natural areas.

COASTS

Just as I have always loved boats, I also love the oceanfront and other waters' edges. They are usually rocky, spectacular vistas, sometimes fearsome, always awesome.

In South Africa, we went out to the Cape of Good Hope, a rocky promontory reaching into the Atlantic Ocean on the Cape Peninsula, near the southernmost point of the continent. There is a museum there commemorating the clipper ships that sailed around it on their way from Europe to Asia before the Suez Canal was built to allow ships to sail from the Mediterranean to the Indian Ocean. The most striking memory I have, though, is of the chacma baboons who are so accustomed to tourists that they overwhelm. They climb on cars and get inside if you don't close the doors fast enough. We saw a baboon looking for food in one woman's open trunk. There was nothing she could do until he decided to leave. People are warned not to eat anything in the area, as the baboons will attack and grab the food from their hands.

Cape Horn on the tip of South America is also striking. In chapter 1, I described the difficulty of sailing from east to west around the horn. But we also climbed up in a blizzard in March (late summer there). Cape Horn is a tall promontory; Cape of Good Hope is a flat expanse of rock with waves powering over it when the winds are high. On another expanse of oceanfront in South Africa live the Cape penguins, little waddling critters that have adapted to fairly warm water compared to Antarctica.

The most amazing islands and oceanfront I have experienced are the Galápagos Islands in the Pacific off the coast of Ecuador. They are volcanic with large expanses of lava. We hiked up lava mountains on Bartolomé Island, which has lava ropes and tunnels. Ships that take passengers to the islands are highly regulated, and only twelve people at a time can go ashore on any island. People must stay on paths at all times to avoid trampling the nests of the many shorebirds that live there.

When we first went ashore, we saw blue-footed boobies a ways off, and of course, everyone was taking photos. Before we knew it, we had boobies around our ankles, up close and personal. They are not bothered at all by humans since we are not predators there. While we were exploring Isabella Island in a panga (dinghy), we were in the middle of a flock of blue-footed boobies who were in a feeding frenzy, dive-bombing all around us. Apparently, we were sitting over a school of fish the birds were after for dinner.

So many other birds, seals, and iguanas are all around. The sea lions pile up on the sandy beaches, so I decided a group of seals should be called "a slither of seals."

We met Lonesome George, at the time, the oldest living giant tortoise. The Charles Darwin Research Station on Santa Cruz Island keeps track of animals and their behavior to observe evolutionary changes and to minimize the effect of almost two hundred years of human disturbance. They collected tortoise eggs and raised them in pens for two or three years because they wouldn't survive predation by the wild pigs and rats on the island. Non-native feral mammals

off the ships of the explorers in the 19th century have multiplied and will kill and eat the eggs. Scientists are trying to
eliminate the invasive animals, but some of the islands are
covered in wild growth, where goats and pigs can hide. They
tag a "Judas goat" to lead hunters to the herd so they can be
eradicated. I recently heard that they have found baby tor-
toises in the wild for the first time in decades, meaning their
efforts to eliminate the rats and wild pigs are succeeding.

The guides are alert to changes of behavior by the endemic
animals. One day while we were watching a short-eared owl,
a flock of storm petrels chased the owl. Our guide made a
note of that, as ordinarily, the owls go after the much smaller
petrels, and they had reversed their behavior. We also saw
a frigate bird chase a tropic bird and pull his tail until the
tropic bird squawked and dropped the fish from his mouth,
which the frigate bird then caught! Each day, we visited a
different island to see the birds that had evolved separately,
like Darwin's finches, with beaks developed to eat the particular seeds that existed in their habitat. Ecuador, which
includes Galápagos, has more species of birds per size than
any other country. It was easy to see why Darwin's theory of
evolution developed after seeing how different species developed differently by being isolated in unique environments.

Another amazing coastline is in Nova Scotia, the Bay of
Fundy. It has the highest tide in the world, about forty feet!
Boats tied on a dock at high tide are hanging in the air when
the tide goes out. Bill and I drove to see the tidal bore, when
the incoming tide crashes against the outgoing river and creates a huge pile of water. The massive outgoing tide leaves

a lot of bay bottom exposed, which is where most of the sea scallops of North America are harvested.

The Atlantic coast of Ireland is also spectacular. The Cliffs of Moher were carved by millennia of wave and wind action. You can still look down and see the sea beating against the cliffs and feel wind so strong that it is hard to stand there and not be blown away. More about my exploration of Ireland in chapter 5, "Trains, Bikes, and Automobiles."

* * *

Closer to home, the sand dunes on the east shore of Lake Michigan are also awesome. My family was staying near there one summer when my mother was alive. We decided to hike the trail to the top, about half a mile up. My nephew Curt stayed at the bottom with Grandma to look at the wildflowers. While we were sitting on the top of the dune looking at the spectacular view down the cliff to the lake, along came Curt and my mother, who was eighty-nine and had also just climbed the whole way up! Is "intrepidness" inherited?

The shores of Lake Superior are also pretty spectacular. On the south shore is Pictured Rocks National Lakeshore, a cliff of many colors caused by water exposing the various minerals in the rock. It can only be seen from the lake, so it is necessary to take a tour boat or kayak out to see them. When Richard and I wanted to rent a kayak to do so, we were told we had to take a half-day training before we would be allowed to rent the kayak because Lake Superior can change from calm to wild in a short time. Since we only had a half-day, we settled for a tour boat. The North Shore of Lake Superior is just as stunning, with powerful, wind-driven waves crashing against rocky cliffs. When we camped in the Northwoods as a kid, it was fun to take a side visit to my uncle's summer home on the top of a Lake Superior cliff beside a rushing stream. I also remember my father daring us to stand in Lake Superior at a calmer spot by Duluth long enough to read the Sunday "funny paper" on the bottom. The water was clear and ice-cold, and we came out with numb legs and feet!

I am less excited about beaches but have had fun playing in the surf. On Kauai, Hawaii, I body-surfed with my granddaughter. In Florida, I enjoyed walking Pensacola Beach with my sister, who used to spend a couple of months there to get away from Michigan winters. Beaches are places to relax; rocky ocean coasts are places to be awed.

GARDENS AND PARKS

Perhaps the least adventurous of my nature travels are visits to gardens and parks. As a gardener, it is always special to see spectacular public and sometimes private gardens. The epitome came with a garden tour of Southern England with my horticulture instructor from the Morton Arboretum. She had received her horticulture training in England, so she knew many of the gardens and gardeners for us to get private tours.

England has estates with professional head gardeners who design and manage a team that takes care of acres of plantings. We were able to visit Stourhead, a 2,650-acre estate in Wiltshire, where we had a guided tour of the extensive gardens. Another day, we had tours by head gardeners at Hidcote Manor and Kiftsgate, English gardens with both formal "rooms" carved out from hedges and wildly informal beds with riots of colors and plants in masses.

The highlight was attending the Chelsea Garden Show in London, which takes up a huge arena and open areas around it. I was particularly impressed by the American native plants exhibited by the Garden Club of America, displaying wildflowers that they had cultivated. Familiar woodland plants from my own garden, such as different species of trillium, were obviously fertilized and grown with TLC, so they were huge and much bigger than they become in their natural habitats. Of course, there were extensive exhibits of single species, such as roses or chrysanthemums, more than one can take in on a single visit to the show.

* * *

Another beautiful garden experience was to the tulip festival at the Keukenhof Gardens in Amsterdam in April, with acres and acres of beautifully landscaped beds of tulips and other spring bulbs. They are so focused on tulips that the gardens are open only from April through June when all the various species of tulips are blooming. Wendy and I even bought a little pot of tulips to put on the windowsill in our stateroom on the boat we were taking through the Netherlands. Tulips are grown for their bulbs, which are sold all over the world.

* * *

The first formal garden I visited years ago was the Butchart Gardens in Victoria, British Columbia. Wendy and I were fascinated and wanted to see it all while our husbands waited somewhat impatiently. Victoria is on a peninsula surrounded by warm ocean currents, which allows many plants to be grown farther north than would be the case inland.

Since that time, I make a point to visit gardens wherever in the world I am traveling. I am less enamored by the formal gardens in Italy and France, like the Luxembourg Gardens in Paris, because they may have a few flowers planted, but mostly, they are walks through open areas landscaped with grass and some trees. In ages when most of the population lived crowded in city blocks with no greenery, these were indeed areas to enjoy for an outing. France does have some spectacular gardens to rival any in the world, though. The formal gardens of Versailles and the gardens around some of the châteaus on the Loire, like Chenonceau, were marks of wealth by royalty who had gardeners, along with their huge staff, to manage them. A garden with a significantly different style is at Giverny, just north of Paris, which was Monet's inspiration for his paintings of water lilies and flowers. Visiting Giverny in bloom is like a walk in an Impressionist painting!

In the US, I have had the good fortune to visit Washington, DC, for the Cherry Blossoms Festival. It's hard to plan in advance because they may bloom anywhere from mid-March to mid-May, and the flowers last only a couple of weeks. They surround the Tidal Basin (near the Jefferson Memorial) and reflect on the water, making an even prettier show. The DC cherry trees were a gift from Japan many years ago and have become a spring spectacle worth a trip to walk around the basin, seeing the trees in bloom and their reflection on the water.

* * *

In Kauai, Hawaii, we visited the Limahuli Garden, the National Tropical Botanical Garden. They have reconstructed the ingenious system used by the first inhabitants, Polynesians who came by canoe in about 200 CE, so it is called the Canoe Garden. They brought plants with them and divided the island, so each tribe had its own section, from the mountains down to the sea. Each of the communities was self-sustaining, and their use of the land was sustainable over hundreds of years, until the mid-20th century.

I am lucky to live near the Chicago Botanic Garden, established at the beginning of the 20th century and a treasure just north of the city. My mother, who grew up in Chicago, remembers taking the train with her father to visit the Botanic Garden. Also in Chicago, the new Millennium Park has the Lurie Garden, which was designed by internationally noted Dutch garden designer, Piet Oudolf, using native plants. He designs in the style of Jens Jensen, a Danish-American landscape architect, who, in the late 19th century, advocated for using locally native plants instead of importing exotics, which were the fad then. In fact, I live about a mile from the Jens Jensen Preserve in Deer Grove, the first urban forest preserve in the US.

You can see that I seek nature in its many environments, in my travels, and in my life. It is one of the driving forces for my travel. I do like cities, as I write about in the next chapter, but I seek ways to be on or near the water, in the woods, in the mountains, or just in a garden. Years ago, I was in a group where we discussed what gives us joy. One of my answers was being in nature. Still today, that is in my awareness. Whether walking in my yard when the spring ephemerals are blooming or in dense woods or a blooming prairie in August, or seeing the spectacular color in the fall, nature brings me joy. My soul is nourished in these places.

"There are no words that can tell the hidden spirit of the wilderness, that can reveal its mystery, its melancholy, and its charm."

—THEODORE ROOSEVELT

Chapter 4

PEOPLE AND CULTURE

"Fear is for people who don't get out much."

—RICK STEVES

COUNTRIES HAVE PERSONALITIES

One of the inspiring things about international travel is to experience the differences among countries and their citizens. There are some characteristics that stand out in third-world countries, but cultures go deeper than that and indeed define the character of a people. A goal wherever I go is to meet local residents and experience some of their ways of life, to get past the surface presented to tourists. I always choose to stay in locally owned hotels, inns, or B&Bs. I don't find value in going to a foreign country and then staying in an American hotel.

I use the word *culture* without a capital *C*, meaning not just the arts and promoted events, but the embedded approach to life and living, the way people treat each other and visitors. Sometimes the culture is apparent immediately and proves not to be just a first impression. Other times, it is more subtle and takes a combination of observations and experiences to form a clear perception, particularly when there are contradictory elements. For example, some places I have visited are both friendly and rude, or are cold initially but warm up after knowing people better.

I start this chapter with the countries that most positively impressed me. Then I write about countries that have characteristics that set them apart but are not necessarily representative of the whole culture. Finally, I write about some elements of culture that are so negative, they override the positive qualities of that country in my experience. Then I will group some key elements of culture, like food and garbage.

NEW ZEALAND

At the top of my list of countries with a welcoming and kind culture is New Zealand. We didn't have any negative experiences there on either island, which differ significantly. Even when bad things happened, like experiencing an earthquake, the response was so helpful that it became another indication of a strong, positive culture. I was impressed with the way the government includes and fairly treats the indigenous Māori population. It wasn't always that way, but in the late 20th century, they passed a law that credited the Māori owners of the land that the British had usurped so that current buildings have to pay rent to the rightful landowners. The nation celebrates the Māori culture, using both languages on signs, and maintaining native community meeting houses, which were and still are used for entertaining, for funerals, and for religious and political meetings. They are a focus of tribal pride built with distinctive, beautiful architecture and carved totems.

The country and population are also very environmentally conscious, which is built into all their practices. The South Island is a jewel for outdoor enthusiasts. Kiwis, as they call themselves, treat visitors with welcoming kindness and honesty, and the country is immaculately clean. Everyone takes pride in their country.

Our group experienced three examples of incredible caring and honesty. One woman in our group used her iPad as a camera. At one point, she left it where she had been sitting on a park bench in Wellington. When she discovered it was missing, she told our guide, who called the police department, and sure enough, someone had found it and turned it in!

My friend discovered when we got to our hotel in Queensland that she had left her little purse, which held her passport and money, in the seat pocket of the plane we took from Auckland. She told the desk agent at the hotel, and he immediately got on the phone to Air New Zealand to track it down. It took a while to get to the attendants on the specific flight we took, but he kept calling until they found it and had them set it aside. Then he went in the cab with Barb back to the airport to make sure she got it back.

My own experience was leaving a package I had bought at the museum gift shop at the top of the teleferique to the Botanic Gardens. The gardens are on the side of one of the mountains that Wellington is built on, and we rode the tram up but walked down through the gardens. We were mostly down in the rain when I discovered that I didn't have my package. When we got back to the hotel, I called, and sure enough, they had found it and set it aside for me to go back up the next morning and retrieve it. We found that if we were standing on the street looking at a map, someone would stop and ask if they could help us find our way.

We were on the west side of the South Island when an earthquake hit Christchurch on the east side. We weren't in any danger but felt the tremors. The next day, however, we were headed to Christchurch. Our hotel had lost power and with the ground moving and things akilter, they couldn't run the elevators until they had been realigned, so they kindly moved our rooms from the fourth floor to the first and carried our luggage for us.

My total experience in New Zealand was wonderful. The beautiful country is taken care of by everyone. They show fairness to all the population, friendliness, politeness, and honesty, the apparent lack of racism, and the progressive laws. I decided if I ever moved from America (and lately, I feel like I might need to with our culture degrading so badly), it would be to New Zealand.

AUSTRALIA

In second place, I think, is Australia. Also very polite, articulate, and helpful, but with some serious problems. Sydney is built on a sprawling harbor, so instead of buses, you get around on ferries. Not knowing my way around, I would ask the ferry ticket sellers how to get to where I was going and always got friendly, clear directions. (I compare that to trying to find my way in Chicago by bus, where the drivers don't want to talk to you, and if you ask if they are going a certain place, they act offended and mumble something without looking at you.) Everyone I met in Australia was friendly and polite, except a Pakistani cab driver, who definitely was not representative of the culture.

My concern about the treatment of the Aborigine population left a negative impression of the country. I learned that sellers of amazing Aboriginal art on the street have bought it from the artists with a payment of maybe a sandwich and a cigarette for days' or weeks' worth of effort. But Australia does have government stores that sell native art—paintings, baskets, and fabric. They cost a bit more money, but they pay the artists a fair amount, so I felt better buying items from those stores. I treasure my pottery with their stylistic "Dream Weaver" patterns of Aboriginal art.

I was working in Sydney for a couple of weeks, so I stayed at an apartment hotel in the city and walked to and from the office with locals. I was able to experience the vibe of the city, and I found the Aussies to be polite and pleasant, even in their hurry at rush hour. I explored the city alone in the evenings and never felt in danger or had any concern about pickpockets or other problems. Sydney became one of my favorite cities in the world (along with Chicago and Paris!).

FRANCE

Third on my list is France. That may be because it is the country I know best after the US. I like France for different reasons than New Zealand. It is a beautiful country that appreciates and celebrates its history, its art, its food, and its joie de vivre. France used to have a reputation of being rude to tourists, but the president a couple of decades ago told his people that tourism was their biggest industry, and their reputation as unfriendly or downright rude was hurting their economy. He expected them to change their attitude and behavior toward visitors. They did! The difference between my experience in the 1960s—when my husband got his hand slapped for taking a Coke out of the cooler—"It's not self-service!"—and the 2000s was amazing. I speak French, but sometimes when I am searching for a word, I am asked if I speak English, and their English is better than my French, so they are happy to speak it.

Paris exudes such a positive vibe. I love walking around and taking the Métro just about anywhere I want to go or taking friends to some of my favorite places. My son and daughter-in-law lived in Paris for two years for their jobs and became Parisians. They went to bistros for dinner at 9:00, sat in sidewalk cafés, walked in the beautiful park across the street from their apartment, and they too loved the city. I studied French in college but then didn't use the language for many years. I have friends who taught French, and both had lived in France more than once during the summers. But I had never had the opportunity because it didn't fit my life or career.

When I retired and became a widow, I finally took advantage of a program to live in Paris for six weeks and take classes to improve my French. In addition to daily classes, we were also coached on how to move past the careful pronunciation of students and sound more like the French with our language. We also had guides each Friday who were experts in some notable places in and around Paris, which allowed us to get insights and details most people would never learn about famous sites.

Staying in an apartment hotel, I was able to have breakfast in my suite, so I could shop like the French and buy my fresh baguette each day. The small group that made up my class ate lunch out most days, exploring many different cafés and parts of the city. One of the women in our group became our "tour guide," with a new suggestion each day for a concert or out-of-the-way museum. If I was studying in the evening, I could shop at a market and prepare dinner with my stovetop or microwave.

I loved every minute, except I was there in 2015 when terrorists bombed the stadium and a restaurant and tried to bomb a concert hall. I lived near the hospital where they took the victims and heard the sirens before I knew what had happened. We were safe in our apartment hotel but were told not to go out until the police had things under control. The next day, Saturday, the city was quiet as people mourned, and the Métro was closed. I walked over to the square, where a spontaneous memorial was built with flowers for the victims.

My son and daughter-in-law, who worked at the US Embassy in Paris, had a ticket for me to join them at the Ambassador's Ball with the president of France and other dignitaries. I had packed a formal dress and accessories and was excited to be part of the event, but it was scheduled the day after the bombings, so of course, it was canceled. The terrorists' intent was to disrupt the Parisian lifestyle, and they succeeded, but only briefly.

I have always found the French helpful. When my granddaughter was eleven months old, her mother had a conference in Paris and didn't want to leave Libbe home with a babysitter that long, so having just retired, I went along to Paris as her nanny. I had a little collapsible stroller, but it was a challenge to carry her and the stroller down the stairs to the Métro. (Paris is not handicap-friendly!) But I always had offers from kind strangers to carry it up or down the stairs. Libbe had just learned to say hi, so when I carried her in my back carrier, she waved and said hi to all the crusty, old French men who smiled and said *bonjour* back.

Last year, when I led a group of friends to France for a barge trip, we started in Paris. I made the mistake of thinking we should take the Métro to where the van was picking us up, which required a change of trains (instead of taking taxis). Schlepping our luggage, this time old ladies instead of an infant, we had offers of help from strapping young men.

I have not found a part of France that I don't like. Provence has its special light, as many Impressionist painters celebrated, and a charming lifestyle that is contagious. I loved driving around Provence and the Côte d'Azur, ending with a week at a beautiful house near Avignon that my friend had rented and invited us to stay. I share more of this trip in chapter 5, "Trains, Bikes, and Automobiles."

Normandy is poignant with its museums and cemeteries commemorating the loss of life from the Allied invasion in World War II. The symbol of Normandy is the poppy, which grows wild there. It was made famous by the poem, *In Flanders Fields* written by John McCrae during World War I. The poem describes the poppies blooming between gravestones. Poppies are considered the battlefield flower because they are the first to grow back after war pockmarks the landscape.

I love poppies, so when my group was visiting Bayeux, where

the famous tapestry from the medieval time is on display, I noticed a shop nearby called *Coquelicot*, which means Poppy. I had to explore it because all their products are created by the owner, who is an artist. I bought a vase and some other items with poppies decorating them. As I was paying, I turned around and—voilà!—I saw my son and daughter-in-law and their friends. They were living in Paris at the time, but to be in Normandy at the same time as I was, and in Bayeux at the same time and even in the same shop was an incredulous coincidence. Turns out, Steen took his group there after visiting the museum to look for a Christmas present for me since he knew I love poppies! But seeing that I had already bought lots of poppy items, he didn't have to, and so my present that year was something different.

I loved taking a trip up the west side of France, which is rural but cosmopolitan at the same time. We started in Toulouse, a part of France I had not been to. Carcassonne is a medieval fort still in use on the French-Andorra border and interesting to explore. I also describe a driving trip from Strasbourg through the Alsace-Lorraine to the Rhine in chapter 5, "Trains, Bikes, and Automobiles."

As I wrote in chapter 2, I have skied in the French Alps at Trois Vallées (Courchevel, Meribel, Val Thorens) and Morzine. The snow is never as good as the American Rockies, but the ambience and food are superb, and the Alpine towns are charming. It's a different kind of ski experience than the American West.

THE NETHERLANDS

Another country with a welcoming personality is the Netherlands. Perhaps not as ebullient as the French, the Dutch are ultimately practical and logical, hardworking, and open-minded. Typical of their attitude was a comment by the Dutch prime minister when the immigrant situation in Europe became so political. He said, "You are welcome here, but please don't expect us to change our culture. We have nude beaches, and if you don't like that, don't go to the beach." He also said to his fellow Dutch about going to the beach, "Please dress for the body you have, not the body you wish you had!"

When I was working in the Netherlands, my client invited me to her home in The Hague. As we toured the city, I wondered about the government buildings in the 1950s, which stood out in contrast to the handsome 16th-century stone buildings in Brussels. I was told that these buildings were hastily built after the city was ruined by Nazi bombs in World War II. The Hague was and is the seat of government and is also the headquarters of the International Court of Justice and was a strategic position for the German army. There are some impressive buildings left standing, such as the Noordeinde Palace, the Queen's home, but it's striking how much damage was done, and half a century later, it's still a reminder of the devastation of war.

I experienced Dutch kindness when my friend Wendy and I took the train from Amsterdam to my Dutch friends' home one Sunday. There was no agent in the terminal, so we tried to buy tickets from the machine, but it wouldn't accept our credit cards, which was before the US had cards with chips. So we got on the train expecting to pay cash for a ticket on the train. When the conductor came around, I explained the situation. He said it usually costs twice the ticket price to purchase on the train, but he would just charge us the regular price. He admonished that we would have to purchase return tickets before getting on the train. So returning, my friend went to the station with me and used his card to buy a ticket, for which I reimbursed him in cash.

In Amsterdam with Wendy, we considered renting bikes and joining the Dutch in their preferred mode of transportation. However, we decided that it would be dangerous. Crowds of bikers in the bike lane were whipping along, and not knowing where we were going, we would be obstacles if we paused or rode at all tentatively. There are more bikes than cars in Amsterdam, all the streets have bike lanes, and there is a huge parking lot by the train station that holds only bikes. Women bike to work wearing heels and skirts, and men in suits, and people carry all sorts of things on bikes.

We took a tour boat on the canals instead and saw the classic

Dutch architecture while moving leisurely along on electric-powered boats. No gasoline engines are allowed for the same reason that they greatly reduced pollution from cars. As in so many things, the Dutch are way ahead of most of the world in preventing some of the damage from climate change. The technology of their dikes and contemporary seawalls and floodgates will probably be an example for other sea-level countries.

POSITIVE CULTURE IN OTHER COUNTRIES

A number of other countries I have visited are welcoming and have vibrant cultures. In Ireland, traveling with my sister, brother, and sister-in-law, we were tracing the roots of my maternal grandmother. While we had some stories from my mother and knew some of the locations to explore, we found a genealogist in County Offaly who was very generous with her time. I learned that each county in Ireland employs a genealogist because so many Americans go there to trace their ancestry. We loved the outgoing, helpful owners of the inns where we stayed. My sister-in-law has celiac disease and must avoid all gluten. We discovered that Ireland has the most people with that diagnosis of any country in the world, so all restaurants are required to post which dishes are gluten-free and are very helpful and concerned to serve clients appropriately.

Each of the Scandinavian countries has its own culture, and all are cheerful and welcome visitors. My husband's grandfather came from Denmark, so when we visited on our honeymoon, we were treated like royalty. They all spoke English because, they said, they couldn't travel anywhere else in the world and expect others to speak Danish. I have

been back since and find the Danes to be pleasant and efficient. I respected them greatly when I learned that during
the second world war, the invading Germans required that
Jews wear black armbands, so the Danish king and citizens
all wore black armbands to show their support.

Norwegians love their country and are proud to show it off.
They value their spectacularly beautiful country and work to
keep it so while ensuring that visitors are treated cordially.
Swedes love their country too and are open to immigrants
and are not prejudiced against other religions or nationalities.

In other parts of the world, I have had equally cordial wel-
comes. I was impressed with the Vietnamese. They welcome
Americans, in spite of the damage done to their country
by what they call "the American war." Poor or not, they are
gracious and generous. Approximately 50 percent of the
population were not alive during the war, but many have
suffered as a result, have lost parents or grandparents, and
had their culture significantly changed by Communism.
Newly allowed, they now embrace entrepreneurism. Even
in Hanoi, now the capital of the country, they proudly show
off the grand boulevards and handsome buildings from
French imperialism, though that was a difficult period in
their history.

In Bulgaria, I visited with my son and daughter-in-law, who
were on assignment there for three years. We drove around
the countryside and were welcomed by B&B owners. In one

beautiful inn in the countryside, the proprietors only spoke Bulgarian, of course, and my son spoke enough to communicate. They laughed when I said the only words I knew in Bulgarian were *merci*, which they actually borrowed from the French, and *Schmatka*, the name of Steen and Kristi's cat, which means, roughly, "dumbass." Bulgaria is a poor but proud country. Steen had studied Russian, which is similar to Bulgarian, but as he was learning Bulgarian, his tutor said he spoke Bulgarian with a Russian accent, and that was not good! I was impressed that after the end of the Soviet Union, the city of Sofia gathered up all their Russian statues, and instead of destroying them, moved them all to a park outside the city. Yes, that was their past, but they didn't need to honor those invaders in their lives today.

In Thailand, we saw the extreme contrast between Bangkok and the rural areas. In the countryside, we stayed in a small resort run by a Muslim family. They invited us to a traditional dinner in their home, where we sat on the floor (a custom so the hosts would never run out of enough seats for all their guests). The husband and son ate with us while the wife cooked in the kitchen and served course after course to us in the living area. We ate with our right hand only, used a finger bowl, and made sure not to show the soles of our feet, which is an insult to those facing us. I also learned not to take the last bite of food, as leaving a clean plate indicates that you were not served enough and invites a second serving.

In very crowded Bangkok, we became more typical tourists, visiting the Buddha statues, temples, and bazaars. We were there on Diwali, staying on the Chao Phraya River, for the Hindu festival of lights. Diwali symbolizes the spiritual "victory of light over darkness, good over evil, and knowledge over ignorance." Light is a metaphor for knowledge and consciousness. Everyone buys little handmade boats of Styrofoam with leaves and candles that are lit and set afloat after dark with a wish. It is beautiful to see all the lights floating down the river. I was concerned, though, about all that Styrofoam floating away and was assured that little boys in boats go out the next morning to collect them all.

Buenos Aires, Argentina, is a vibrant city. We enjoyed strolling, stopping to see the spontaneous tango dancers on the street, and the colorful architecture of La Boca, where houses were traditionally painted with leftover paint from the ships anchoring in the harbor nearby. One house could have a different bright color on each wall. Traveling to Patagonia, we experienced the contrast between the estancias (massive ranches on the Pampas range) and the spectacular Andes Mountains. We hiked a bit in Tiera del Fuego National Park before getting on the expedition ship to round the Horn (as I wrote about in chapter 1, "Boats"). I learned that the Andes range runs the length of South America, and it is the same geological range that runs along the Antarctic Peninsula and onto the continent. It's geologic proof that all of the continents were once connected.

My latest visit to an impressive country was Morocco. I loved the culture, which is secular Muslim, with an ancient history of nomadic Berbers, who lived there for centuries before the Arabs overran it in the Muslim expansion of the 10th and 11th centuries. The Mediterranean coast was part of the Roman Empire. Some Roman ruins were excavated in the early 20th century, under a 14th-century Muslim necropolis called Chellah that was built over them. After that, Morocco was invaded by the English, French, and Spanish. The area along the Mediterranean has the Andalusian influence from the Spaniards, and the rest of the country has the French influence. Morocco gained independence from France in 1956, but the official languages continue to be Arabic and French. It is ruled by a king, but during the Arab Spring in 2011, instead of an overthrow that happened in many other Arab countries, the king responded by making some much-needed reforms to education, healthcare, and other services. The citizens are devoted Muslims, and you hear calls to prayer several times a day, and most women wear hijabs (scarves) but not complete burkas. Men wear street clothes and often djellabas, which are loose robes worn over their pants and shirts. Women are gaining some rights that are not granted in some stricter Muslim countries like Saudi Arabia.

I expected Marrakech, an ancient city with a walled Medina of winding, narrow paths, to be crowded and chaotic like Cairo, but I was pleasantly surprised by how beautiful and clean it is. There were wide landscaped boulevards, gardens, and parks that reflected the French influence. The Djemaa El Fna square *is* crowded and full of vendors and food stalls, snake charmers, motorbikes, and donkeys, but no cars. You go there to wander, shop, and look. The rest of the city is safe and beautiful to walk, or to take a horse-drawn caléche ride, or to go to museums and mosques.

Another ancient city is Fez, with the largest Medina in the world of narrow alleys that don't allow cars. There are miles and miles of winding, convoluted paths that are impossible to navigate without someone who knows their way around. We tried with one woman in our group using a GPS to find our way, but it didn't map all the little alleyways, and we got lost. One can find anything possible to buy: cow and sheep heads that people cook and eat, spices, every vegetable, olives, dates, all sorts of household items, and of course, tourist souvenirs. But no liquor or wine (which is available in the newer part of the city).

NICE PEOPLE, TROUBLESOME CULTURES

I have been to many countries where the presenting culture is annoying or otherwise unpleasant, but where the individuals we met were gracious and welcoming.

Egypt and especially Cairo are extremely crowded and dirty with aggressive vendors, whose approach is to cheat tourists. Vendors are at every monument, visitor site, and market. Our guide said at the outset that we should not try to negotiate with vendors because even if we think we are getting a good deal by negotiating from twenty dollars to ten dollars for something we want, it is only worth two dollars, and we will be the "catch of the day" to a vendor. Our guide said to tell him what we want to buy, and he would negotiate a fair price for it. Another tactic: a vendor approached me with the iconic carved cat statues for one dollar, so I said I wanted four for little gifts for my cat lover friends. He gathered them up, wrapped them, and I gave him the equivalent of four dollars, but he said that, no, they were ten dollars each! I was angry and wasn't going to pay that, but Ali came along and scolded the vendor, and we walked away. I asked why the vendor did that. He lost a sale, but apparently, the approach works most of the time.

That type of aggressiveness is rampant in the traffic, too, with drivers, buses, bikers, and pedestrians all crisscrossing the roundabouts at the same time. On the other hand, we were invited to lunch with a farm family who prepared a delicious meal from the vegetables they grew and chickens they raised. They had a stack of terra-cotta tagines by the kiln, so I asked if I could purchase one. They said no and gave it to me as a gift. They were gracious, attentive hosts, showing a completely different face than the ubiquitous vendors. Our guides at the magnificent monuments—pyramids, tombs, temples—also showed a different face. They were extremely knowledgeable and were proud of their heritage and glad to share it.

Mexico is another country that presents two faces. The art and Folklórico music are exuberant and beautiful. On one visit to Cuernavaca, I was working with a group of people who were enthusiastic and focused on improving their workplaces. They introduced me to their preferred restaurants for lunch. My hosts were gracious and generous, making sure I was welcomed, taking me to dinner, and introducing me to some special places on the weekend between my two workweeks there. But walking through a neighborhood in Mexico City, I was stepping over rats by the curb that were attracted to the garbage on the street.

I was there a number of years ago, but last year, we planned a visit to Copper Canyon with a Mexican guide my brother knows from a town across the border from where he lives. However, the US State Department warned Americans not to go there because of the drug cartels, so we canceled our trip.

I have had mixed experiences in Italy too. The gorgeous countryside and hill towns in Tuscany, the spectacular Dolomite Mountains, the pride by chefs in their wonderful food and wine, the fun at a cooking class, the amazing Renaissance art, Roman ruins, infrastructure, and more. The general rudeness of drivers and people in crowds shows a different view. I saw cars squeeze through narrow spaces, taking off side mirrors of cars they scraped by. With three friends in Florence, dragging our luggage to the train station, we were accosted by a Romani woman, dirty and aggressive. She shoved an old newspaper at Linnea, whose purse was hanging around her neck in front, and while yelling at us in Romani (I assumed), she pickpocketed Linnea's billfold and passport and ran away. We were in front of a hotel, so the desk clerk was helpful by calling the police and giving us a phone to cancel the credit cards. The police just told us to go catch our train and to go to the US embassy in Rome to get a temporary passport when we got there. I know that one can experience personal crime anywhere, but I have traveled to sixty countries, and that was only one of two times I have been with a victim (also Saint Lucia, see chapter 1). It does leave a negative impression.

Wendy and I went to South Africa in a small group led by two women who lived in Chicago but were from South Africa. It is a country of contrasts. A beautiful country with national parks in the savanna and oceanfront, but it also has slums, "informal settlements" that spread for miles around Cape Town. We were there after the end of apartheid, but the scars remained. Our bus driver said he was "colored" or of mixed race—his grandmother got together with a Dutch sailor. During apartheid, people were forced to live in segregated communities—whites, blacks, and colored. "Colored" also included Asians, Indians, Malaysians, and Chinese who had immigrated over the years to work in the mines and other jobs. The driver said he was forced to move from his home close to where he worked to a town miles away, with no compensation for the home he had to leave. I asked him what would have happened if they had refused to move, and he said the police would have come in during the night and piled their belongings in the street.

We visited Robben Island, where Nelson Mandela had been held with other political prisoners for part of the total twenty-seven years he was imprisoned. The prison now is a museum, manned by former prisoners, and left mostly as it was. We saw the courtyard with some shrubs where Mandela hid the pages of the book he wrote, *Long Walk to Freedom*, while imprisoned. The government made a fateful mistake by putting all the political prisoners together, as they were intellectual leaders and revolutionaries who used the time to plan the country they wanted when they got out while doing manual labor. Mandela was able to implement those plans when he became president of South Africa from 1994–1999.

In Johannesburg, we walked through Soweto, a section that during apartheid had been designated a segregated black community and remains so today. We also went to the Apartheid Museum, which showed the injustice of the system that considered classes of people to be of less value than the whites and the horrible human rights violations.

The contrasts that continue now were apparent when we were welcomed by the brother of one of our leaders to his beautiful home in suburban Cape Town. We had cocktails by his pool, behind piano wire on tall fences. In the country, we were hosted by the parents of the other leader who had a farm in Orange Free State. They offered a sumptuous buffet and barbeque of fresh produce they had grown and raised. It was another example of a beautiful country with significant problems but with kind and generous people.

When I traveled to Turkey, we went a day earlier than the small group started, so we could use miles for our flight. While our hotel in Istanbul was strongly guarded with a scanner to put our bags through, we felt safe walking around Taksim Square, which is considered the commercial center of Istanbul. We took a taxi to the Yerebatan Cistern, an amazing underground water supply with heads of Medusa on columns built in the 5th century to bring water from the mountains to the palace. Then we walked to the Four Seasons Hotel for lunch in the beautiful gardens. The hotel is a remodeled prison, written about in *Architectural Digest* and listed in *1,000 Places to See Before You Die*.

Of course, when we joined the group, our guide assured us that we would not have any concerns about safety, and indeed, we had a wonderful time exploring the Spice Market and the Grand Bazaar, with convoluted paths and hundreds of shops. We also had a wonderful time exploring the ruins of ancient cities along the coast. This was about ten years ago, but today, there is enough unrest in the Middle East that one has concerns about visiting this beautiful, historic country. I wrote in more detail about the gulet cruise along the Turquoise Coast in chapter 1, "Boats," and about the ancient ruins in chapter 6, "Architecture, Archeology, and Artifacts."

THIRD-WORLD CULTURES

I went to Nigeria with a Rotary group to administer oral polio vaccines to babies in some villages near the capital of Abuja. Polio had been eradicated in most of the country, but these small communities had not had people cooperate. In Muslim communities, women are not allowed to let a man into their homes without their husbands present. The country leadership knew that as long as some children were not vaccinated, they could not defeat this crippling disease. Our project was for women in the Rotary team to go out with the male health workers and convince mothers to bring their babies out to receive the oral vaccine.

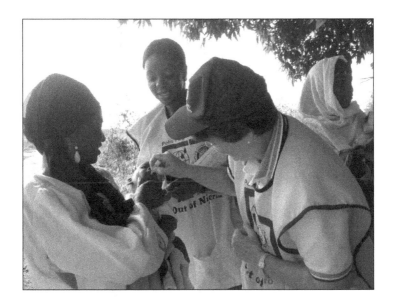

The village leader rode along the dirt roads announcing by megaphone that we were coming. (There was no electricity, let alone radios or TVs to announce the polio eradication campaign.) We met some resistance but were mostly successful. At the end of the time there, we met with the village leader, the Nigerian project coordinator, and US volunteers. The village leader thanked us but asked when Rotary would provide malaria vaccinations.

To that, the project coordinator said, "First, you need to clean the garbage out of your streams and roadsides so mosquitoes can't breed there. Once you take responsibility, we will consider coming back to deal with malaria."

It struck me that the effort to save children from debilitating polio, the free vaccine from the World Health Organization, the major organizing effort by the Nigerian Rotary and government, and American Rotary volunteers was all seen as an entitlement. The good news is that just this year, the WHO has announced that Nigeria is now considered polio-free after three years of no cases. The only countries in the world that still have polio are Pakistan and Afghanistan in war zones that volunteers can't get to. However, our hosts, business leaders in Abuja, were gracious. They put on a banquet of local specialties and were exuberant dancers, inviting us to participate.

The Arlington Heights Rotary Club has built a water pump for the village and funded a school there. We visited the school and brought soccer balls and a pump, which, of course, delighted the kids. Rotary also funds microloans of twenty-five dollars to women to start businesses. Some were able to expand their gardens to raise enough vegetables to sell at the market, and some sewed garments to sell. We had the privilege to attend a passing-on ceremony, where the women, dressed in their finest, proudly told of their success and paid back their loans so the next group of women could benefit from the same money.

* * *

While China is a diverse country in many ways, and I write about some amazing places I visited there, I did have some strong negative impressions. The first came when I got off the flight in Shanghai. All of the passengers on several flights were pushing and shoving in the terminal as if someone was giving away millions of dollars. I was carried along in a sea of humanity, being pushed into the people in front of me, until I was able to see a sign above that said foreigners were supposed to go off to the left. By separating, I could breathe again. All the crowd was doing was turning in their customs form! I kept finding that intense crowd aggressive-ness elsewhere too.

The traffic in Shanghai is the worst I have seen. Luckily we weren't driving. My niece and her husband had a driver to get us around. But drivers, in general, don't pay attention to traffic signals. Most of the time, the city is in gridlock. Bikes and tuk-tuks, cars, and vans are all intermingled.

In Beijing, at the Forbidden City, the rooms that are off-limits to visitors are visible through glass walls. I was standing in front of one, looking through the glass, when a Chinese woman behind me shoved me so hard my face smashed against the window. I turned around and shouted, "There's no room!" I got her attention even though she didn't understand what I said. With one and a half billion popu-lation, they are so used to being in overwhelming crowds that I guess they just learn to push and shove everywhere.

The vendors in public places like Tiananmen Square were aggressive too. They follow you around, and even when you say no, they push their wares in your face. My great-niece, who was studying Mandarin in school, was with us, so I asked her how to say, "I don't want it." I said that to some of the vendors, who were surprised enough to back off. My niece was annoyed that so many women would come up and stroke her little blond daughter's hair. I have been in Communist Vietnam but didn't have the same reaction I had in Beijing. We had hired a driver and guide who spoke English, and when I asked her how she liked being a guide, I got a memorized party-line response. It was obvious she was not allowed to share a personal experience, even if she had a positive answer.

GARBAGE

I believe that a definition of third-world countries is that they don't know what to do with garbage. The difference between a clean country and a garbage-filled one is striking. Singapore is known for its cleanliness: the streets and countryside are pristine. They even have a law against chewing gum so as not to have black sticky spots on sidewalks. Then we drove across the border to Malaysia, and immediately, the roadside was covered in litter. Our bus driver even threw his trash out the window once we got across the border! We stayed in Malacca and took a boat ride on the river that runs through the town. Homes are built on the banks, and residents just throw their sewage and garbage into the river. It was filthy and smelled bad. I think it's a double problem. There are no systems to collect garbage, so people have no way to get rid of it other than to dump it anywhere.

Just like the garbage-filled streams in rural Nigeria, Egypt's streams are plugged up with refuse. The Nile is kept relatively clean because of both commercial and passenger boats, but other waterways are incredibly garbage-filled, to the point of not having any water visible, looking like one could walk on it, though who would want to try? Driving back to Cairo from the Aswan Dam, our bus had a problem, so we pulled off the road. The driver determined the problem and dug through the garbage all around to find some wire to temporarily hold something together. I guessed that whatever he might have needed could have been found in the trash that was everywhere. At least in that case, it was useful!

In Trinidad, we stopped by a wooded area for bird-watching but had to step around discarded car parts, toilets, broken furniture, etc., even though there was a sign posted that said no dumping. In contrast, Tobago is very clean. When I asked about the difference, I was told that Tobago gets funds from Trinidad, the more commercial island, and hires a cadre of government workers, whose job it is to clean the roads and parks. Tobago has more tourists. Is that cause or effect?

Years ago, when we visited Venice, I was excited to see the city on canals, but I was appalled at the garbage floating on their iconic feature. Photos were complimentary because the sun sparkled on the water, but while riding through in a gondola, the garbage had to be pushed aside.

The rats I mentioned on the streets of Mexico City were there, of course, because garbage was thrown out at random with no apparent way to be collected.

In contrast to these observations, New Zealand is immaculate. As in any country that values its beautiful cities and countryside, there are neatly covered bins for garbage and apparently a way to empty them regularly. Along with garbage bins, there are recycling bins placed usefully around the cities and public places as well as in hotel rooms. One doesn't see garbage in the fjords of Norway, on the banks of the Grand Canyon in the US, on the Loire River in France, on the rivers or oceanfront in Ireland, on the tundra in Alaska, or Churchill, Manitoba, or many other places I have visited. I have not been to India, and one reason is because I know I would be repulsed at the volume of garbage I've seen in photos.

FOOD

I am not an adventurous eater. Growing up in Minnesota in

the 1950s, we did not have the variety of seafood, for example, of the coasts. My mother would not buy fish because she said it was "old." Before refrigerated cargo planes, if it had come from one of the coasts, it *was* old. The only fish she would cook was lake or stream fish my father had caught that morning on camping trips. I distinctly remember enjoying certain seafood for the first time as I visited coasts.

One summer in college, I taught swimming at a camp in Maine. With another counselor from Maine, we went to the ocean one weekend and bought lobster fresh off the boats, just boiled. We sat on the shore with a bottle of melted butter. I had never liked lobster in Minnesota when we would have a special dinner, such as after prom, but fresh lobster in Maine was wonderful.

A similar experience was with my husband and friends off the coast of Washington on a fishing trip. We caught our limit of salmon in the morning and cooked it on the campfire that evening. It was a completely different food from the canned salmon my mother bought in Minnesota. Even the salmon we had canned at the cannery on the shore and shipped home was better. Though commercial salmon boats iced their catch, it was not canned for several days after it was caught.

I learned to eat locally grown or caught food, but I still have reluctance over exotic foods.

* * *

On a ferry from Denmark to Sweden years ago, they served a magnificent smorgasbord, but there were so many strong-smelling fish I couldn't eat—lutefisk, sardines, smoked herring, and many I couldn't even identify. In England, we saw whitebait on the menu, and our Dutch friends who were there said that was a good appetizer. So my husband ordered it, and it turned out to be whole minnows breaded and fried. They ate the whole thing, head and all. I define my reluctance as not liking to eat a whole animal! (That includes clams and oysters, and I like lobster tail and claws but not the innards.)

However, I have experienced new food I did like. In England, I had roast beef with Yorkshire pudding, and I came home and learned how to make it, which my boys grew up liking. I also like Dover sole, which I order in both the UK and US. At a pub in the country, I ordered a pot pie made of local game. My cynical husband said that meant they went out in the alley and shot some rodents! When I ordered beefsteak and kidney pie, he asked, "Do you know what kidneys *do*?" In Wales, I had the best fish and chips I've ever tasted. We bought fresh-caught cod that was batter fried and served in a paper bag with French fries. We sat on the shore and enjoyed both the food and the view.

In Australia, after a busy workweek, my clients took me to a great seafood restaurant they loved. There was a great table of appetizers, and all the locals swooned over a huge bowl of whole baby octopus. I demurred. I have had raw, marinated octopus legs in a salad in Italy but can't think of eating the whole animal. I was quietly repulsed by a big goblet of seafood my brother-in-law ordered in Shanghai, which had heads and legs hanging over the edges. In Sydney with friends, we went to a recommended Chinese restaurant and were the only non-Chinese diners there. So we asked the maître d' for recommendations. One of the dishes he suggested was "dove" (we thought it was pigeon). While waiting for our order, we watched a man at the next table take the head of the dove by the beak and chomp down on it, bones and all. I don't know if the waiter saw our reaction, or maybe knows that Americans don't like the idea of eating the bird's head, but when our order came, it was carved, and the head was removed!

In Hong Kong, I went to lunch, again with local clients. They were all Chinese except me, and ordered for the whole table and shared, as is typical of Chinese restaurants. I ate things I would not have ordered: thousand-year eggs (preserved in urine!) and eel, but it was cut up and fried, and thankfully accompanied by lots of vegetables. When it came to dessert, they ordered fruit for me, as they said they didn't think I would like their dessert. They were right because they had a bowl of black soupy goo. I think it was seaweed, and they use very little sugar in anything.

I am not a fan of sushi. I have tried things like California rolls, made with cucumber and crabmeat, both of which I like, but still, I didn't like it. As much as I like salt, seaweed is too salty, as is caviar.

We were traveling down the Mekong River in Vietnam and stopped for lunch at a restaurant on the shore. The appetizer that was served for the group was a whole fish fried standing up in a rack, like the British toast racks. It was cooked with coconut, which looked like maggots on the outside, but everyone used their chopsticks to pull pieces of fish off. Once I got past the head and skin, it was good.

I did discover *phở* in Vietnam, which they eat for breakfast, lunch, or dinner. It is a clear broth with chopped raw vegetables and sometimes includes bits of meat and noodles. That is a discovery I have cooked at home since then, and when I visit my son in Silicon Valley, California, we often have lunch at a Vietnamese restaurant so I can get genuine *phở* (pronounced "fah"). The area has many ethnic restaurants, especially Asian.

* * *

In China, with my niece and her family, we took day trips

from Shanghai with their driver. One day as we were getting ready, Julie made sandwiches to take. When I asked her why we wouldn't just eat at a restaurant for lunch, she said she didn't trust the local food. When we got to the little town to visit, I saw why. A woman from a restaurant that backed up to the river was washing lettuce in it! On a trip to Beijing, we had dinner in a restaurant that had its own fishpond outside. As we walked across the bridge, seeing the fish swimming, Jim asked his five-year-old daughter which fish she wanted for dinner. When we looked at the menu, she said, "No fish, Mama, no fish!" I think she thought we would eat it alive! We ordered Peking duck, and she thought it was a peeking duck. She also thought it would be a live duck. At the time, she was a very picky eater, as are many five-year-olds, but now as a young adult, her tastes have broadened, perhaps because of all their international experiences.

Closer to home, in New Orleans for a conference, I was determined to at least try crawfish. At an upscale restaurant, I ordered a Cajun crawfish dish and didn't like it. Thinking it was because I am not crazy about Cajun, the next night I ordered crawfish étouffée and still didn't like it. I gave it a fair trial, but at least I didn't act annoyed at a whole crawfish used as a garnish on other dishes, as some of my companions did.

In Belgium with an international group, the Scandinavians who spoke several languages didn't speak French. So they asked me what *tête de veau* was. I said it means "head of veal," but I didn't know just what kind of a dish that was. One of the Belgian hosts said, "Oh, you don't want that!" Turns out, in English, it is headcheese—a pâté-like dish made of the meat scraped off the face of the calf. Another common dish in Belgium is *moules frites*—a bowl of mussels in the shells with French fries (and mayonnaise!). When Wendy asked for catsup with her *frites*, they charged her a euro for a little packet!

On the other hand, there were several popular dishes I liked. In the spring, they harvest white asparagus, and every restaurant advertises its special dishes made with white asparagus—white asparagus with seared scallops, truffle-marinated white asparagus, tuna salad with grilled asparagus. I also discovered fruit beers, which any beer lover would cringe at, but not being a beer drinker, I was fine with raspberry beer!

Working in Mexico, we went to a late lunch each day. I learned that Mexican tacos are not at all like the tacos we have in the US, other than the corn tortillas. We would order several types and share—fish and cabbage, pork and mushrooms, chicken and cheese, etc. Never hamburger with lettuce and tomatoes!

Sailing in the Caribbean, we learned to have the chartered boats partially provisioned because the availability of groceries in the little towns and beaches was limited. We discovered food we hadn't seen before, like little black balls about the size of a softball we knew were either fruit or a vegetable. Turns out, when cut open, they were watermelons! Chartering in Saint Lucia, literally a banana republic, we were provided with a huge stalk of bananas for a week. In the heat, they ripen quickly, so we concocted lots of ways to use them—banana bread, banana pancakes, banana cocktails (with rum!).

* * *

Sailing in Tonga, on one island, we attended a Tongan feast put on for tourists. There was a long table with food spread out on large palm leaves. My granddaughter, who was eight, was turned off by the suckling pig with the apple in its mouth and didn't like the fish or squash, so she ate watermelon. Plates were palm leaves, and we ate with our fingers. The pork and vegetables were actually very good. After the meal, we were entertained by Tongan dancers. The men do a warlike dance to drums, and the women do a dance similar to the Hawaiian hula, and then we were invited to join them.

* * *

In Nigeria, the local Rotary group put on a great dinner for us American guests. They eat lots of meat—beef, lamb, and chicken—and serve yams in many forms. They are not the same vegetable we call sweet potatoes. They're blander and in need of sauce or lots of spices. Another night, we went as a group of about fifteen by bus to dinner at a steak restaurant. Our reservation was for 7:00, but we were seated at 8:00. Almost everyone ordered steaks, which were grilled near our table. Some customers got served around 8:30 and others later and later. Three of us were still waiting, and when we asked about our food, we were told it was next, while the first served were done and ready to go back to the hotel. Thirty minutes later, I finally went over to the chef to complain, but apparently, women aren't supposed to do that. We were finally served at 11:00 p.m.!

* * *

One needs to try poutine at least once in Canada. A huge plate of French fries is covered with melted cheese and gravy. We learned to order one serving for several people as an appetizer and still have some left over. It must have two thousand calories *if* someone could eat the whole serving! My favorite meal to order in Canada is pickerel. In the US, it is called walleye but usually comes from Canada or Northern Minnesota. It is a flavorful, mild fish like Dover sole.

* * *

I loved the tagines in Morocco. A tagine is a terra-cotta cooking dish, and also the way food is prepared in it. The base can be from six inches to maybe eighteen inches across, always with a conical lid, often attractively decorated. The food is carefully arranged with, perhaps, chicken at the base and vegetables propped against it in a pyramid, accompanied by a sauce of spices poured over it and then baked. I liked it all so much, I bought some tagines to bring home as gifts and for myself. I also bought some Moroccan spice mixes of cumin, ginger, coriander, and saffron.

* * *

Of course, the food is great in France and Italy, but most noteworthy in Italy are the liquors. After a ski trip, we were at dinner in a restaurant owned by a friend of one of our group. He was being a cordial host and provided us with complimentary grappa. It is made from the grape skins left after the wine is made and is so strong I can barely touch my tongue to it, let alone drink it. On the other hand, I discovered Limoncello, which is a good aperitif.

My favorite cuisine is French, both in France and in the US. I like small portions with a variety of tastes on the plate. I love the presentation and the wonderful sauces. The best fish I like to eat is in French restaurants, often served with a lemon-butter sauce. On the barge trip on the Loire Canal in Central France, each day we had a gourmet lunch, including a cheese course. The chef chose two cheeses each day from a different region in France. I am not crazy about strong hard cheeses, but I did discover a new soft cheese I really liked called *Époisses de Bourgogne*. It has a texture like Brie, but with a different flavor. When I got home, I tried to find it in stores here and did discover it at Whole Foods, but at twenty-five dollars a half pound!

* * *

I am not very learned about wines but have attended wine tastings in several countries—South Africa, New Zealand, France, Germany, Argentina, as well as California and Michigan. I have learned which French wines I like. At home, I buy Marlborough, New Zealand, sauvignon blanc and now know that French Sémillon or Sancerre are similar crisp whites.

I am allergic to the sulfites in red wine, so I usually avoid them, but in the Chianti region of Italy, I decided I really needed to drink some Chianti wine. I did and did not have an allergic reaction, so I thought maybe my allergy was gone. Shortly after that, I was in Bulgaria at dinner with my son's boss, who was a wine expert. She chose a good Bulgarian wine for us. I drank it and had an allergic reaction, not life-threatening, but like an immediate hangover. That is when I learned that the Chianti sold locally in Italy does not have the sulfites added. But when red wines are going to be exported, as the Bulgarian wines are, sulfites are added as a preservative.

There are a lot of cuisines that I have yet to experience, but lest it sound like I am hard to please, I do like foods in each country I visit. I usually come home with a recipe I want to try, sometimes needing to go to specialty groceries to find the right ingredients.

"To travel is to discover that everyone is wrong about other countries."

—ALDOUS HUXLEY

Chapter 5

TRAINS, BIKES, AND AUTOMOBILES

"All who wander are not lost."

—J. R. R. TOLKIEN

TRAINS

I have not traveled extensively on trains but have had some memorable trips. Some have been memorable for their problems, others for the territory they travel through. One trip that has been on my bucket list for years that has not yet occurred is the Trans-Siberian railroad that takes seven days and crosses Russia from Moscow to Vladivostok, 9,258 kilometers (6,152 miles). But that experience will have to wait for another book or as an addendum to this one.

Perhaps the most problematic train trip was in the Czech Republic from Prague intended for the little town of Český Krumlov, eighty-four miles south. Richard and I had flown into Prague, explored for a few days, and then headed to the medieval town of Český Krumlov on what was supposed to be a two-hour trip. All went well until we got about half of the distance, the train stopped abruptly, and the conductor told everyone to get off. It seems that the track was torn up in front of us for repairs! Not that it just happened, but somehow the railroad failed to note that the scheduled train could not get there.

We unloaded with our luggage and walked a block to a bus station so we could finish our trip by bus. We made the connection in time, and the bus got us to the outskirts of the little town of Český Krumlov, where we were dropped in a vacant lot on the hillside. No cabs, no buildings, no information. We traipsed, dragging our luggage down the hill on a cobblestone road to the town.

We found the street of the pension (B&B) where we had reservations, but we couldn't find the address, so we stuck our heads into a realtor's office who luckily spoke English. We found out that there was a lower street, which we were on, and an upper street with the same name where our B&B was located. We had to climb a several-hundred-step path up the steep hill, dragging and lifting our bags all the way. When we got to the lovely B&B, the hostess wondered why we were so late, but she was ready with a relaxing cup of tea for us! We did enjoy exploring the old city and castle the next day, but we took a cab to get there!

* * *

An overnight train from Malacca, Malaysia, to Bangkok, Thailand, was another adventure. With a small group led by a New Zealander, we had "first-class" tickets with sleeper bunks. The sleeper cabins were not like those in the US.

These just had a curtain and were double-decker beds. I had reservations about sleeping in such a vulnerable way on a crowded train, so I buried my purse under my pillow, and we slept in our clothes. We arrived in Bangkok without incident, tired, but ready for new adventures.

* * *

My favorite trains are the TGV in France—*Très Grande Vitesse* (translates as "greatest speed"). This is part of the European high-speed rail system that serves travelers so well. Traveling from Paris to Avignon in Provence, for example, a distance of 689 kilometers (414 miles), takes just two and a half hours! You can get the TGV in the Charles de Gaulle Airport terminal in Paris with no hassle, avoid the city traffic, and get to your destination efficiently. The TGV trains travel on their own tracks with few stops. It does make it hard to see the landscape as you speed by at an average 320 kilometers per hour (200 mph), but the trains are new, clean, and comfortable.

The Paris Métro is the most efficient way to get around the city. When I lived in Paris for six weeks, I bought a monthly pass for the Métro and avoided having to buy a ticket for each trip. You do hear announcements warning of pickpockets on the trains, and I saw one grab the computer bag off the shoulder of a man standing in a crowded car and jump off just before the door closed. A warning bell sounds, and then the doors close automatically after a couple of minutes. People are warned not to try to stop a closing door because they do not reopen. I saw a woman whose face was injured because she tried to jump on as the doors were closing, and they closed on her head and shoulder. They had to create that rule early on because the trains couldn't run on time if every stop was delayed while a door opened for a latecomer.

* * *

All city trains are not as efficient as others. In Washington, DC, I take the Metro from the airport to my son's house in Falls Church, Virginia, and it works efficiently. But one Saturday in 2017, we took the Metro into the city to join the Climate March through DC. It took us a few stops, and then we all had to get off due to repairs being made on the tracks. We were able to catch a bus to get us closer to our destination, but then it was diverted because the streets were closed for the march! We had a bit of a hike to get to the start of the march with hundreds of thousands of other demonstrators, plus the mile-long march itself. My son uses the Metro more often living there and says it is really poorly run and frequently has that kind of problem.

* * *

On a more pleasant note, I have ridden trains because they travel through scenic areas. One took us from Sault Sainte Marie, Ontario, through the Northwoods and along the North Shore of Lake Superior to the Agawa Canyon. There are no roads that go there, so the only way in is by train—or foot! We were able to hike out to waterfalls, have lunch in the park, and hop on the train back to the Soo.

I have also ridden the narrow-gauge railway in Colorado from Durango to Silverton. It is a breathtaking trip that crosses deep canyons on trestle bridges between peaks in the spectacular San Juan Mountains. Built in 1882 to carry ore from the gold and silver mines, it is now only a passenger train on a jaw-dropping route, so you don't have to drive and try to look down the cliffs on every turn.

BIKES

I used to bike a lot more than I do lately. The road I would have to ride on from my house to local bike trails is narrow, and without a bike lane, it's a dangerous undertaking. Since I lost my husband and my good friend no longer rides, I have less motivation to do so. But we had some memorable rides over the years.

Perhaps the most unique was the RAGBRAI—the Register's Annual Great Bike Ride Across Iowa. For forty-seven years, the *Des Moines Register* newspaper sponsors this weeklong ride of almost five hundred miles on differing routes from one side of Iowa to the other. Thousands of bicycle riders participate. Many years ago, my good friend and her family were doing the RAGBRAI, so my family joined the ride too. We rode two days of the distance, starting mid-state and continuing across to the eastern border.

Each day was almost one hundred miles, and as we rode, we talked to various other riders from many backgrounds who came along. One old man I talked with was a local farmer who said last year he watched the throng ride by and decided this year to join in. You meet serious bike riders and others who join for a section just to be sociable. People who live along the route sell or give away lemonade or snacks.

My husband and I and our older son all had good twenty-one-speed road bikes, but my youngest son, who was a pre-teen, was on a smaller ten-speed bike to fit his size, so he had to pedal more to cover the same distance. We traveled seventy-five miles the first day, and as it was getting dark, we decided to get picked up by the sag wagon that traveled the route to help people with problems or who wimp out and want a ride. Competitive Mike objected. He wanted to finish the remaining twenty-five miles (probably another two hours)! We camped in a school gym overnight and started out the next morning with the crowd. The second day was a bit shorter, and we were getting sore muscles, so it was good we didn't try to do the full week's ride.

Another distance ride was the Apple Cider Century in South-west Michigan. It too has hundreds of riders on one hundred, fifty, or twenty-five-mile loops through the countryside. We decided to do the fifty-mile route. There were sag stops along the way, with refreshments of apple cider, fresh-picked apples from the orchards, and a chance to take a break. I was in my forties and was proud of myself for keeping up with a group of young, athletic men who were drafting close behind to help break the headwinds. However, when we came to a steep hill, they easily pulled away from me as I shifted down to make the climb easier, and they continued in high gear!

I have joined several rides in the city of Chicago. Not being a fan of riding in city traffic, I enjoyed these Sunday morning rides with the traffic diverted from the route. One of these was the Chicago Boulevard Lakefront Tour, which started on the Midway Plaisance by the University of Chicago. It progressed around the whole city on boulevards, along the West Side, through neighborhoods on the North Side of the city, through the Loop (downtown), and back down Lake Shore Drive to the starting point. It attracts hundreds of riders and has traffic directors at major intersections as the mob rides through. At the finish line, there are refreshments and even leg massages!

Each Memorial Day Sunday, there is the Lake Shore Drive ride I have participated in for several years. It starts in Grant Park, and we ride along the shore of Lake Michigan on the major thoroughfare of the city, which is closed to car traffic for the morning. This ride is about fifteen miles and takes less than two hours. Sometimes the ride is slowed by the crowd of bicyclers but on a nice day, it's a fun way to see the city and its spectacular lakefront. I have also done one midnight ride through the city. It's a unique ride with no traffic, but not so great for a person who never has been a night owl.

Leading my Senior Girl Scout troop years ago, we did several interesting rides. One was along the Elroy-Sparta rail-trail in Wisconsin. It was the first rail-trail built in the US, fifty-three miles long, and goes through four former railroad tunnels. We camped along the way with our own accompanying van that carried our gear.

There are many other great trails in the Chicago area that I have biked. The Great Western Trail follows the former Great Western Railroad route for about thirty miles through suburbs and out into the pretty countryside. Rail trails are easy to bike because they are relatively smooth (crushed limestone or blacktop) and provide a comfortable width. One runs through part of Palatine, where I live, where the railroad used to bring people from the city of Chicago out to the Deer Grove Forest Preserve, the first such designated urban forest preserve in the country.

My ski club is active in other sports besides skiing, including bike rides along the Fox River and the North Shore bike path that runs through the Chicago Botanic Garden and paths through many other forest preserves. Biking is always a great way to get some exercise while enjoying the countryside.

My one experience on a mountain bike ride was in Sun Valley, Idaho, years ago. My husband attended the National Ski Patrol convention in June, and a group of us decided to rent bikes one afternoon. I had never ridden a mountain bike at the time, and we were with some very experienced mountain bikers. We started high on a mountainside with a foot-wide trail winding through the sagebrush, catching on the pedals. I was on the brakes the whole way, and early on decided to stop and let the guy behind me go on because I definitely was going slower than he wanted to. It was a different experience than my trail and road riding in the Midwest!

Recently, somewhat compromised by age, I was finding it harder on my back to ride with the dropped handlebars, and it became harder to swing my leg over the bar. I also had toe clips with my bike shoes clamped onto the pedals, which required a twist to release them. That meant I had to anticipate stops to quickly release my feet from the clamps. The first time I used them, I stopped suddenly and quickly twisted my right foot off, but the bike wanted to tip to the left, so I fell with my left foot still clamped to the pedal. Luckily, I only had a skinned knee. I got used to the clips and found them efficient for riding, but I later decided it was time to change. So I sold my lightweight skinny-tire road bike and bought an old-lady bike. It has granny gears and a "girl's bike" bar but is heavier, and the tires have more resistance, so it's not as much fun to ride. Hence, more automobile road trips!

ROAD TRIPS IN THE US

When we were a young family, we traveled mostly by car in the US, as do many families. I don't remember any trips to cities, though. As we did when I was growing up, we vacationed in nature, mostly in the West and North. We drove across the country, visited national parks, camped, and hiked. When my boys were young teenagers, we drove to Yellowstone National Park, camped in the national forest on the edge of the park, and drove our van in to see Old Faithful. We parked in the large lot and walked over with the crowd to watch the geyser erupt. When we got back to the van, we saw that whoever was last out didn't even slide the door closed, let alone lock it. We were alarmed at ourselves, but on inspection, all our gear was untouched inside, even with the door wide open. Sometimes you get lucky!

We followed the still-existing remnants of the 19th-century Oregon Trail on another trip to the West. My mother knew a researcher at the University of Minnesota who had written an unpublished guide to where to find the trail, which compared where the trail was in relation to 20th-century landmarks. In some places, you could see the actual ruts across the prairie. In other places, the local roads run on the actual route of the original trail. In some areas, there are gravesites along the trail where pioneers were buried as they died during the long ordeal. The most difficult to learn about is Donner Pass in the Sierra Nevada Mountains, where most of the Donner party died of starvation after being stranded all winter by huge snows. Donner Pass is near Lake Tahoe and the ski areas where I ski, which still today measure snowfalls in feet, not inches. In 2019, for example, Squaw Valley had thirty-seven feet of snow from November to April! It is always amazing to think we can drive across the distance of the Oregon Trail in a few days, compared to the months pioneers took on horseback and wagons and all the hardships they endured.

Other driving trips took us west through the South Dakota Badlands and Mount Rushmore National Memorial and across Montana. It is a good way to understand the huge expanses of the West. One year after a conference in Seattle, we dropped one son off at a ski racing camp in British Columbia at Whistler, where they skied on a glacier in June. Then we drove the distance across Canada, camping along the way, from the incredible Canadian Rockies to the endless expanses of plains in Saskatchewan to the lake country of Manitoba north of Minnesota. One of the most beautiful sights along the way is Lake Louise in Banff National Park. It is a turquoise, glacial-fed lake nestled in the craggy Canadian Rockies.

One memorable trip east was to Virginia and the North Carolina Outer Banks. We saw the wild horses running free, and it was the boys' first experience tumbling in the ocean surf. Our kids became good travelers by having experienced so many vacations with us across the country.

* * *

After I retired, I took a road trip with my friend Liz to the Southwest. We hiked in the Utah National Parks—Canyonlands, Arches, Zion, and Canyon de Chelly National Monument, Arizona. Canyon de Chelly is an ancient Navaho site with prehistoric rock art and spectacular rock formations. Then we drove to the corner of Colorado to explore Mesa Verde National Park, where they allow visitors to climb the cliff dwellings and learn about the ancient Anasazi civilizations. Just south in New Mexico is Chaco Culture National Historic Park with similar cliff dwellings. It is an amazing place, which has the largest collection of ancient ruins north of Mexico. The park preserves one of the most important pre-Columbian cultural and historical areas in the United States. Between 900 and 1150 CE, Chaco Canyon was a major center of culture for the Ancestral Puebloans. Researchers think that the same civilizations created both Mesa Verde and Chaco Canyon, plus another in Mexico, which were all built on the same longitude, sequentially. Why one city was abandoned and others then built may have been because of climate change and the loss of water in the area.

Liz had studied and traveled with experts in the area and made the history and art come alive. She is a potter, and I collect indigenous pottery, so we both enjoyed visiting Native American pueblos to see the experts making their world-renowned pots. Most of my collection consists of museum replicas of ancient art, but the pieces I bought at the Acoma Pueblo are treasured pieces signed by the artists. Read more in chapter 6, "Architecture, Archeology, and Artifacts."

* * *

A fun road trip took Richard and me from Seattle down the West Coast in September to Silicon Valley. Our goal was to visit as many national parks along the way as we could fit in, and to stay in the old historic inns built when the parks were first established early in the 20th century. We spent a few days in the San Juan Islands off the Washington coast, kayaking and enjoying the solitude with calm ocean water. From there, we took a car ferry across the Puget Sound to the Olympic Peninsula. I was glad to revisit and hike again in Olympic National Park and the rain forest of old-growth trees and mossy paths through the woods. As I said in chapter 3, these forests are like cathedrals to me, and it's a spiritual experience walking quietly in them.

We drove inland a bit to Mount Rainier National Park and were lucky to see that the mountain was "out," as it is so often in the clouds. It is one of the tallest mountains in the US at 14,441 feet and has the most glaciers of any mountain in the lower forty-eight states. It is a spectacular view with the snowcapped peaks standing above the rest of the Cascade Range. We hiked in the meadows at the base, but because we were there in September, we missed the alpine wildflowers that are profuse in spring.

In Oregon, we visited Crater Lake National Park, but with

an eight-inch snowfall the day before, we could get to the old inn, but the rim road around the lake was closed. I had hiking boots along but no winter gear, so I bought some knit mittens in the gift shop and managed a short hike in the unexpected cold. The lake is the crater of a volcano that erupted 7,700 years ago and is the deepest in the US, with a ridge around it that allows for looking down into it. A pretty spectacular sight!

From there, we continued down to Northern California and Redwood National Park. We learned that a local group of environmentalists, the "Save the Redwoods League," caused the old-growth redwoods to be saved in state parks in the early 20th century. After 90 percent of the awesome trees were cut, and only because of the state parks, the federal government finally created a national park around the original state parks, with Lady Bird Johnson inaugurating it in 1968. The redwoods are awesome, the tallest trees in the world. They grow to 370 feet tall—as tall as a thirty-five-story building—with massive trunks up to twenty-two feet around and up to two thousand years old! I am sick to learn that loggers are still allowed to cut them for lumber to use for decks and yard furniture. There are only about 2 percent left of the redwoods that were there before the logging that started in the 19th century. The only place in the world they grow is coastal Northern California because the climate conditions are just right for them. The reason they live so long is because they, like cedars, are resistant to insect damage and rot, which unfortunately makes the wood desirable for outdoor use, so it is marketable. Every time I can stand in a giant forest and look up, I am in awe and grateful that some wise people were able to save some of these incredible trees so later generations of nature lovers can be refreshed in their midst.

On this road trip, we continued down through wine country, stopping for tastings at vineyards often and enjoying the fall California sun and local B &Bs along the way. The only way to explore all these national parks and meander through Napa and Sonoma is by a leisurely road trip. There probably will be a few more in my future!

INTERNATIONAL ROAD TRIPS

My first road trip in Europe was on our honeymoon in 1962. It was quite an adventure. We really didn't know a lot about what we were about to do. We flew on the cheapest airline (not even a jet) to Scotland, traveled by train through Scotland and England, then across the English Channel on the rough ferry ride I described in chapter 1. When we got to Le Havre, France, we took a train to Wolfsburg, Germany, to pick up a new Volkswagen Bug to drive ourselves around Europe. The car cost $1,350, a bit more because it had a sunroof! Friends of ours were traveling in Europe too and also bought their Volkswagen at the factory.

We drove together from there to Berlin, which was behind the Berlin Wall that had just been built. To get to Berlin, we had to drive through Checkpoint Charlie, have our papers and cars inspected, and wait to be allowed to enter. As we stood on the West Berlin side of the wall and looked over, I heard "Achtung! Achtung!" It was someone yelling at us that we were too close to the wall and could be shot! Innocents abroad! We drove near the Brandenburg Gate between West and East Berlin, which was the only opening in the wall. Wendy and I got permission from the guard to drive our car behind the Soviet monument and up to the wall about a block before turning around to come back. Our husbands, not knowing we had permission, were livid that we dared to drive there. Other than angry spouses, we were all fine.

We had so little money that we followed a popular book of the time called *Europe on $5 a Day*. I remember seeking a restaurant called Aushingers, where we could get a recommended bowl of bean soup for thirty-five cents. To be sure, these were 1962 prices, but still the type of bargain we were looking for. After our cheap lunch, we indulged in German *apfelstrudel* at a little bakery.

From Germany, we drove to Denmark to visit Bill's relatives. His grandfather had come to the US from Horsens, Denmark, so we were able to visit his great uncle and his family. A second cousin just a bit older than us was named Steen, which we decided was the name for our son a few years later. Unfortunately, over the years, we lost track of the Danish relatives. Steen tried to track them down years later, but there are a lot of Simonsens in Denmark.

We continued to cover as much of Western Europe as possible in eight weeks. We drove south through Germany, where we experienced the Hofbräuhaus in Munich. I have never been a beer drinker, but I did manage to down one of the huge mugs of noncarbonated beer with the locals cheering me on. We drove through some of the quaint villages in Bavaria, where the underpowered little car had a challenge climbing the mountain roads. We traversed the Alps in Switzerland, Austria, and Northern Italy, held our breath as we drove on the Italian roads with aggressive drivers yelling at us as they passed on curves, and occasionally stayed in youth hostels to save money. Some hostels were decent, but others were iffy. They had dirt floors with straw and wooden bunks. After staying in one of those, we decided to stick to pensions and little hotels, mostly walkups, but clean and in neighborhoods we wanted to explore.

My favorite country, of course, was France. I had studied French and the culture in college and was anxious to practice the language and see all the sites I had read about. I was, and still am, enamored with Gothic cathedrals. I had studied art history in college and was mostly interested in architecture, so I was in awe of any of the cathedrals we visited. (More about these in chapter 6).

A memorable mountain experience was going up the Aiguille du Midi, standing on a crowded teleferique tram from the French resort town of Chamonix. It attains a height of 12,600 feet in about an hour. I became sick from the quick change of altitude and felt faint, but I couldn't sit down, so a kind lady gave me smelling salts to revive me. It worked, so when we got to the top and walked around on the glacier in the fresh air looking across the valley to Mont Blanc, I revived.

On that trip, we also visited some of the chateaus along the Loire, again finally seeing some of the French history I had studied. Seeing the lavish living quarters of royalty from the 17th and 18th centuries helps one understand the inequality that led to the French Revolution. That summer, we also visited Belgium and Liechtenstein, the smallest country in Europe. We determined then that nine countries in eight weeks was not the way we would travel in the future. All my travels since then have been focused on one or two countries on each trip. That has allowed me to experience more of the culture of the places I visit and to have time for active exploration.

* * *

Traveling in Italy with three friends, I had another driving adventure in Europe many years later. We rented a car in Florence and drove out to our *agriturismo* (tourist cottage on a farm) and up to the hill towns in Tuscany. We made the mistake of renting a car without automatic gear, which neither of us drivers had driven for many years. I learned the hard way not to shift into second gear going slowly in traffic up a hillside. The car would die, and while managing the brake, clutch, gas, and hand brake with cars honking behind me, I would try to get it started again. It took a day to learn that in those situations, I had to shift into low gear, even while moving slowly. Growing up driving a shift car, one could only shift into low while standing still. We survived but had lots of adventures.

Driving in Florence, we tried not to get into the old city with narrow lanes and no place to park. But one day, somehow, when I got off the main highway, we found ourselves going down a one-way lane so narrow that we had to fold in the side mirrors to keep from clipping them off. A policeman stopped us and asked what we were doing there, and all I could say was we had driven there by accident. We pleaded for him to give us directions to get out instead of getting a ticket. He granted our wish, and we were able to park outside of the old city center and explore the area by foot.

One day when Liz was driving on a roundabout, she hit the curb and, a block later, had a flat tire. We were so lucky that a tire dealer was just down the street, so we were able to buy a new tire and have it put on. Before GPS on phones, we had paper maps, but the roads named on the maps didn't have corresponding signs on the country roads, so we found ourselves in the wrong place often. I did love the little hill towns in Tuscany, each with its own personality and some off the beaten path enough not to be invaded by buses of tourists.

* * *

The UK is another difficult place to drive because of driving on the "wrong" side of the road. Thankfully, I have not needed to be the driver, as I was with Bill one time and Richard a couple of other times. I was working in Basingstoke, southwest of London, so Bill came over and explored Greenwich and the seaside by himself for a few days. When my workshops were over, I joined him. Driving in England works better with a driver and a navigator, but not always smoothly. Particularly when driving on the opposite side of the car, on the opposite side of the road, turning the opposite way on roundabouts, it takes the concentration of two to navigate. Then there is the issue of reading signs to know which exit to take! Sometimes we went around twice to figure it out. My friend Wendy's husband, Scott, used to call her the "nagrivator"! We did get to see some areas on my list I've longed to see—Stonehenge, the Cotswolds, the original Gothic cathedrals in Winchester, and Salisbury. (More in chapter 6.)

Driving in England and Wales with a GPS caused different problems. Richard was doing the driving, and we called our English-speaking GPS "Gypsy." Sometimes when I was reading a low-tech map, Gypsy would be telling us to go one way, and my map said the other way. Richard said he couldn't have two mistresses! He was good at staying on the correct side of the road but remained white-knuckled on narrow lanes with high hedgerows when he couldn't see trucks bearing down around the corner. We were staying with friends who had rented a house for two weeks, and one afternoon, when it was our turn to cook dinner, we were following Gypsy, who took us around barns, through cornfields on one-way paths, and got us lost. The group had to go out to dinner, as we didn't get back in time to cook!

***

In Ireland, my brother was driving. I was in the front seat with him, trying to program the GPS, his wife was in the back seat with Google Maps on her phone, and my sister was also in the back with a paper map. And they didn't always agree! I could get us to the next town but couldn't get the GPS to get us to the hotel or the site we wanted to get to. Carol's Google maps did, but often with a street name which, of course, we couldn't see until we were at it. In Ireland, my brother Rich was a trooper driving, but he wanted clear directions, not the name of a street, not knowing which way to prepare to turn. Otherwise, it was a great trip.

We started in Dublin, where our favorite museum, Dublinia, portrayed Viking history in Ireland, and of course, we ate in an Irish pub. It seems like every country I have been in has at least one Irish pub—including the coast of Thailand!—so it was fun to eat in an actual one in Ireland. One of our goals in Ireland was to do some genealogy. Our grandmother had come to the US from Offaly County, so we spent some time there. We knew the town, Tullamore, and manor house where she had worked as a cook, so we were able to find those. When we went to Tullamore and said she was a Malloy, the response was that everyone in the county is a Malloy!

We drove to the West Coast and explored the moors of Connemara National Park, Galway Bay, and a great oceanfront at the Cliffs of Moher and the Ring of Kerry. We were there in September, and it rained every day. The week after we left, Ireland actually had a hurricane hit the coast, driven up the ocean current from warmer water. We loved the friendly people and got good advice for places to stay, as we didn't know in advance how far we would get each day. A highlight of our stay in Killarney National Park was a recommendation by our inn owner when we asked where to go for dinner. He suggested the Muckross House because that evening, they had a band and Irish dancers, so we enjoyed impromptu super entertainment for the evening.

I enjoy exploring medieval castles, and Ireland has the most castles of any European country (estimated at thirty thousand!). This includes the ruins of ancient fortifications against the Vikings and other raiders, as well as medieval castles built by Irish and British noblemen as protection from invaders by sea. We had a chance to tour the medieval castle in Bunratty and attend a medieval banquet with madrigal singers as an example of 16th-century entertainment.

We skipped Blarney Castle, with the throngs of tourists hanging backward off the parapet to kiss the Blarney stone, said to give them the gift of eloquence. Kilkenny is also a medieval city with a beautiful castle. We had dinner at a pub that is rumored to have been the hangout of a 13th-century witch. Who knows the accuracy of these myths, but I am always impressed that normal buildings from seven centuries ago are still in use, especially compared to old buildings in the US, less than three centuries old, which are usually torn down.

* * *

I have had several road trips in France. Richard's daughter lives in Alsace, so he had visited often and had gotten used to driving in France. The roads are better than in the US, and of course, not driving on the left side, as in the UK, makes things easier. Driving in Paris is crazy, as it is in most big cities, but Richard was good in the traffic. On one trip, we flew to Paris, took the TGV to Avignon in Provence, and rented a car there. Trying to find our hotel in the old city with narrow lanes was a challenge. We went around and around, finding the street but only finding it one way—the opposite way from where we were. We finally asked someone how to get to it and were told that we had to drive along the sidewalk and plaza to enter the road from the right direction! When we did get to the hotel, there was no place to park, so we unloaded our luggage and took the car to a parking ramp a few blocks away. By that time, it was pouring, so we got soaked walking back to the hotel. After that, we learned not to stay in the old part of towns if we were driving.

We spent a week driving and exploring the Languedoc region

and the Cote d'Azur. We loved Nice but parked on the street by the hotel and found the window broken when we went out in the morning. We had to spend most of the morning driving out to the airport to the car rental agency to exchange the car. The car had an obvious sticker in the window telling thieves that it was a rental car, so they broke in, expecting to find valuables left in the car. We didn't leave anything in the car, so the vandal did not get anything for his efforts to break in. We asked the agency if we could take the sticker off the window, but they said no, so the next night, the break-in happened again! Once again, the rental agency exchanged the car, but then the hotel finally told us not to park on the street but at a car park ramp nearby.

There are some spectacular areas of Southern France that most tourists don't get to. An area called the Grand Canyon of France, the Verdun Gorge, is not as big as the Grand Canyon in Arizona, but it's a mile deep with a turquoise river running through it and has amazing views. There is also the red city of Roussillon (with all buildings made of red clay) and others that are off the beaten path and awesome. It is fun to wander little towns and talk to locals who are not swamped by tourists. One of my favorite stops on that sojourn was Saint-Tropez on the Mediterranean. We walked along the dock and saw the yachts of the rich and famous, and I was just a little jealous that I was not on a boat.

Our friends had rented a country house near Avignon, so it was fun to join them for camaraderie and some local excursions. We went together to Arles and the Roman amphitheater and to the old town of Les Baux-de-Provence, with a castle built on a towering rock that was impossible to be attacked. We explored the medieval village of Èze, with its winding, narrow streets on a steep hillside, and Le Village des Bories, now a historic monument of conical houses of stone built without mortar. Since taxes had to be paid only on dwellings, the residents dismantled their houses to a pile of stones the day before the tax collector was coming and built them up again the next day!

Of course, I love the fields of lavender that Provence is known for and that Cézanne painted, but being an archeology buff, I thoroughly enjoy exploring medieval sites too.

The Western side of France was another area that I had not visited before. We started in Toulouse in the southwestern corner of the country. On our first night after getting off the plane, we wandered through the town square and came upon a flash mob—a group of singers who gave a spontaneous performance for whomever happened to walk by. They had wonderful voices, and it was a fun way to be welcomed to a new city.

We explored Carcassonne, a 13th-century fortified city that is still intact and has the longest walls in Europe and a full city inside. It is on a hillside in Languedoc on the Canal du Midi, a strategic position for protection during a time of raids. It has recently been designated a UNESCO World Heritage Site. We walked the cobblestone streets and had lunch at an open-air restaurant, a contemporary experience in an ancient environment.

That same trip took us north through the Dordogne to the town of Sarlat, another well-preserved medieval town. It has more registered historic sites than anywhere else in Europe! Most of these towns from feudal times had a castle with a lord providing protection in exchange for the labor of the vassals. Some have new cities built in the valleys around the castle, but some have stayed the size they were when they were built five or six centuries ago.

For years, I had wanted to visit the caves of Lascaux. They no longer let visitors into the original caves, trying to preserve the art by Stone Age dwellers from seventeen thousand years ago. But there is an exact replication built into a cave nearby, with bulls, wild boar, deer, and other animals painted on the walls. It is just amazing to me that we can actually see art created by people from that long ago.

In the same area, we took a short cruise on the Dordogne River through the land ruled by Eleanor of Aquitaine in the 12th century. We drove north to the Loire Valley and the town of Saumur with cobblestone streets and half-timbered houses before getting to Château de Chenonceau, one of the famous chateaus on the Loire, built in 1515 with construction overseen by women, which was unheard of at the time. Diane de Poitiers was mistress to Henry II, and his wife was Catherine de' Medici. They both had bedrooms there at the same time! I am more fascinated by medieval times and architecture than by the later chateaus, but they do give a glimpse into the lives of the ruling class from that period.

* * *

Richard and I took a road trip from Alsace-Lorraine, which is now part of France, to the Rhine River Valley and up to the Moselle River. Alsace-Lorraine has been a pawn between Germany and France over the centuries, changing countries after wars and acquisitions. Richard's daughter lives with her French family in Strasbourg, which is a charming medieval city with a Gothic cathedral. We rode bikes through town with a family that uses bikes to get around as we use cars in the US. Strasbourg was known for its Christmas market, until recently when concern for terrorist attacks caused the city to cancel it. The recent introduction of COVID-19 hasn't helped.

When we started our drive, Richard asked me how many castles I wanted to visit, and I said, "All of them." I didn't know at the time that the Rhine has a concentration of castles with thirty-nine along about one hundred miles of the river from Mainz to Cologne. We looked at most on the rocky promontories along the way and visited several. Most were built in the 13th century by local royalty to collect duties from anyone who traveled along the river below. In the 17th century, the armies of Louis XIV raided, ended the lucrative toll system, and damaged most of the castles.

In addition to our drive, we took an excursion boat for a section of the river, so we could see castles on both sides. The most renovated and lived in is Burg Eltz, which is on the Moselle River. The tallest of the area castles was built in the 14th century and has been in the same family for hundreds of years. The present heir lives there and greets tourists as visitors to the period-furnished rooms that have bouquets of flowers she arranges. Walking the bridge across the canyon to the entrance, one can appreciate the secluded site, protected from attacks.

There are appealing little towns along the Rhine as well. Rüdesheim, though very touristy, is quaint. Rothenberg is the best-preserved 14th-century town, with half-timbered houses that have overhanging second stories and narrow cobblestone streets. It's easy to imagine life there six centuries ago. Visiting some mountainside vineyards along the way, I learned about halbtrocken wine. I like white wine, but not as sweet as most Rieslings. I discovered that halbtrocken means "half-dry," which is much to my liking. We made a point to drive to Cologne to visit the massive Gothic cathedral there, which I will comment about more in my next chapter on architecture, archeology, and artifacts.

However I travel—on boats, trains, bikes, by foot, or automobiles—my goal is not just to see destinations but to experience them. That way, rich opportunities provide rich rewards and many memories.

"Thanks to the Interstate Highway System, it is now possible to travel from coast to coast without seeing anything."

—CHARLES KURALT

Chapter 6

ARCHITECTURE, ARCHEOLOGY, AND ARTIFACTS

"Feeling awe is the true feature of health and happiness."
—ANONYMOUS

When I was studying art history in college, I was always most interested in architecture. I loved every era and the type of architecture that was the icon of its time. Since I live near Chicago, I can feast on the city's magnificent architecture. Chicago became a showcase for architecture after the fire in 1871 when architects from all over the country came to help rebuild. The city reflects the history of modern American architecture, from the skyscrapers first built in Chicago in the late 19th century to present-day spectacular contemporary architecture. It has served as the showcase for noted architects from Daniel Burnham and John Root to Louis Sullivan and Frank Lloyd Wright in the early 20th century to Mies van der Rohe, with his Chicago School midcentury, to Skidmore, Owens & Merrill, Frank Gehry, and Jeanie Gang, in the 21st century.

Architecture continues to be an interest, and it is supported by much of my travel. I am glad to have some background in painting and sculpture, but I have never been as fascinated with that as with architecture.

GOTHIC CATHEDRALS

It is hard not to feel awe when seeing a soaring Gothic cathedral. I am not a religious person, but I do experience spirituality as I stand in a soaring space looking up. It always amazes me that these spectacular buildings could even be constructed in the 11th and 12th centuries, let alone built to last over one thousand years! The only tools they had were hand tools and buckets—no cranes, and only basic mechanics. Think of that. When peasants were living in thatched-roof huts with dirt floors and barely eking out a living, these magnificent buildings were being built. It is not surprising they inspired wonder and awe. I think the best tangible thing Christianity has contributed to mankind is Gothic architecture! Peasants thought these wonders were miracles, and so do I!

One of my favorite historical novels is *Pillars of the Earth* by Ken Follett. It's about a master builder (like today's architects) in England just as these churches were being designed and built in the 12th century. The main character travels to France to see and work on the first Gothic cathedral built—Basilica of Saint-Denis—now in a suburb of Paris. Saint-Denis was a bishop and the patron saint of France, who was beheaded in 636 at Montmartre in Paris. The myth is that he walked carrying his head to the spot where he wanted to be buried, the chapel of Saint-Denis (spelled Saint-Denys at the time). The cathedral was completed in 1144. It is the church where all French kings and queens from the 10th to the 18th century were buried, and the carved sarcophagi fill much of the nave now. Saint-Denis represents the first use of Gothic elements in its architecture as a distinct break from Romanesque, which has lower, heavy walls and few windows compared to the soaring spires and walls and stained-glass windows of Gothic architecture.

I finally got to Saint-Denis when I was living in Paris in 2015. We took the train out to the tough suburb, which is not considered safe. But the cathedral square is just a block from the train station, so we made the trip and explored the magnificent cathedral and had no problems. However, the next day, November 13, was when the bombings occurred in Paris. The police were all over the town of Saint-Denis, where they determined the terrorists were from and captured two of them.

I wish I could revisit all the Gothic churches in their order of construction to see the evolution over time. The cities competed with each other for who could build the tallest, grandest church until they got so tall that the architecture had to be modified to support them. That is when the flying buttresses were added to support the walls that became less structural because the many stained glass windows and vaulted and ribbed arches replaced round ones to bear the weight of the stone walls and spires above them.

When I first went to Europe in 1962, the first Gothic cathedral I saw was the Milan Cathedral in Milan, Italy, the third-largest Gothic cathedral in the world. It was built a bit later than some, started in 1386, and was continuously built over centuries, so it became more ornate with "a forest of spires" as Gothic style evolved. The stone carvers obviously had enormous skill to be able to create the bas relief sculptures on so many cathedrals. The art of stained glass evolved, too, as that became a new way to teach the Bible to illiterate churchgoers. It is a prime example of Italian Gothic.

From Milan, we went to France, and of course, the top of my list was to see Notre-Dame in Paris, which was started in 1163 but not finished until 1345. It had all the characteristics of Gothic architecture in one building for the first time. The ingenious flying buttresses were grooved to carry rainwater from the roof and spewed out of the mouths of gargoyles. Without these, rainwater running down the sides of the building would seep into cracks and expand when frozen. I have returned many times to Notre-Dame, with two distinct experiences. One was when I was studying in Paris in 2015, and we had the opportunity to visit Notre-Dame with an expert in medieval architecture. I learned much more about the details of the famous cathedral than I had known before, such as the carving of both the angels and devils on the arches and that the Gallery of Kings with forty statues forty feet up on the facade were originally painted.

The famous rose window is the largest in the world, and it was an amazing work of art and engineering to have been built nine hundred years ago! Apparently, Notre-Dame was being neglected until the 19th century, when Victor Hugo wrote *The Hunchback of Notre-Dame*, which became a bestseller. That caused an awareness that renovations were sorely needed, so some of the embellishments of the cathedral, like the spire, were 19th-century additions.

The last time I went to Notre-Dame was in the summer of 2018 when I took a group of friends to experience the interior. That was significant because the next year was when the roof burned and crashed into the interior, forever changing this magnificent landmark. I have not been back since, but perhaps when I can return, some of the damaged roof will have been restored.

* * *

After Saint-Denis, the French excelled with Gothic cathedrals. In fact, 1100 to 1300 CE is called the Age of Gothic Cathedrals. Another spectacular one in France is Chartres Cathedral, which is southwest of Paris. It was built on a hill in the 12th and 13th centuries with a nave the equivalent of twelve stories tall! Approaching it through the narrow streets of the medieval village, you see the church towering above everything. No wonder the religious people of the medieval times risked their lives to make pilgrimages to these amazing tributes to God. The purpose of these cathedrals was to connect heaven and earth. Chartres is the best preserved of the early medieval churches and is now a UN World Heritage Site.

Amiens Cathedral, in Normandy, was built from 1229–1270 and is the tallest cathedral in France at 371 feet! It is hard to believe that this height could be reached without today's construction equipment, such as cranes. Amiens claims to have the head of John the Baptist in its reliquary, brought back from the Crusades in 1204. Of course, these relics brought pilgrims and money to help maintain the cathedrals and the towns around them (and enrich their bishops), so they promoted them to encourage the religious to come. I don't need to go looking for a relic; the cathedral is spectacular from outside and in.

In the centuries these magnificent cathedrals were built, the Virgin Mary was gaining importance in worship, often as an interceder with God. Many cathedrals were named Notre Dame, Our Lady. After Paris, the cathedral in Reims, Northeast of Paris, was also named Notre-Dame. Built in the 13th century, it is considered High Gothic and is incredibly ornate. For one thousand years, starting with the church that preceded the existing one, it was the cathedral where all the French kings were crowned. Another Notre-Dame is in Strasbourg, Alsace. It was completed in the 15th century, but only has one tower and not a central one. At the time, it was considered the tallest tower in France. When we visited Richard's daughter and her family in Strasbourg, we were able to have a local's tour of the magnificent cathedral as well as the medieval town. People who live with these icons take them for granted, but I am always awed. Again, looking at it makes one incredulous that this level of architecture, sculpture, and stained glass could be created at a time when most people were living in desperately poor conditions.

Mont-Saint-Michel is another spectacular medieval church and abbey in France. It was built on a huge rock off the coast of Normandy in the 8th century. Most of the massive abbey is Romanesque with thick walls and round arches, but the present-day church was added in the 12th century, so it is Gothic with soaring arches and huge windows. For centuries, pilgrims trooped there but could only arrive at low tide, as it was inaccessible when the tides came in. That, plus its perch on a rocky mountain, helped the fortress around the abbey repel invaders. In the 19th century, a road was built high enough to be above the tide, so now tourists throng there. It is quite a climb up the mountain and then up the hundreds of steps to the church on the top, but both the architecture and the view are worth the effort.

I planned a return trip to France in 2020 to visit one of the Gothic cathedrals I had not seen, which is in Beauvais in Normandy. Saint Pierre Cathedral was completed in 1172, pushing the limit for taller, thinner walls, which proved unsupportable. In 1284, its tower collapsed from vibrations from strong winds, so it was rebuilt with wooden supports inside, plus iron rods outside, marring the image of freestanding stone walls. That trip was to be spent with my son and daughter-in-law, who also love France, and to visit some medieval villages and castles along the coast of Brittany. Sadly, the shutdown from COVID-19 caused that trip to be canceled.

* * *

Simultaneously to France, in England, cathedrals were being built in the English Gothic style. One of the oldest is Canterbury Cathedral, started in 1070. It had been a monastery from the 6th century, so it had several buildings on the site that culminated in this spectacular cathedral. It is also a United Nations World Heritage Site. These UN-designated sites are designated for a reason, so I make an attempt to see them whenever I am in the vicinity, and they are always amazing. Traveling in 1962, Bill and I took advantage of local docents for sites like this. We had a very informative tour of the cathedral, with explanations of how the church was built nine hundred years earlier and the detailed sculptures and stained glass. This added to my knowledge of Gothic architecture and sparked my continuing interest even more.

In London, Westminster Abbey is famous for the coronation of English monarchs over the centuries. It was started in 1066 by William the Conqueror, who came from France. Of course, he had to have an equally spectacular Gothic building. It was a monastery first and evolved into a cathedral and place of burial of noteworthy British leaders. In addition to looking up at the soaring ceiling and stained glass windows, one looks down at the grave markers underfoot for a history of the country.

In England on a business trip in the 1990s, I made a point to visit another English Gothic monument, Salisbury Cathedral. It was built from 1220–1258, relatively quick compared to some that took centuries to complete. In *Pillars of the Earth*, Salisbury is in the vicinity of the fictional cathedral that the builder came back from France to build. It is considered the finest example of English Gothic architecture and holds a copy of the Magna Carta, signed in 1066. Still today, Salisbury is out in the country southwest of London with the town grown around the cathedral. When one goes to Salisbury, it is to see the cathedral and nearby Stonehenge.

In the same region of England is the Winchester Cathedral of the Holy Trinity (popularized by a pop song in the 1970s). The original church in the countryside of Winchester was built on a hill in 642, so when the cathedral was built in the 11th century, in a valley for protection, the bones of Saxon kings were moved to the mortuary chests in the cathedral. It, too, is huge, with the longest nave of any Gothic church. I enjoy walking in the same area as people from centuries ago, and I try to imagine how they related to these magnificent works of art.

Another great cathedral in England is in York. On a trip to Northern England with Richard in 2011, in addition to the Lake Country, I had to visit York to see the cathedral. The medieval town is charming, but the main draw for me was York Minster, which started in 1100 but took 250 years to complete. It is the largest Gothic space in Europe—525 feet long (one-third longer than a football field!), and it's the height of an eight-story building. One tower is twenty-one stories! We toured the interior with a very knowledgeable docent who had great stories to tell. One I remember was in a chapel where there were gargoyle-type carvings around the top of the walls. The stone carvers could create faces as they pleased, some carving themselves or leaders in the town. One particularly ugly face was a caricature of the unpopular queen at the time! Stonemasons are still employed to maintain all the carvings. The minster was originally built in 627 for the baptism of Anglo-Saxon King Edwin of Northumbria. York is an ancient city. Roman Emperor Septimius Severus ruled the entire Roman empire from here from 208–211 CE.

In addition to the Gothic cathedral, the other architecture of note was the construction of castles with walls around them as forts, and half-timbered houses, some of which still stand. It is fun to find and explore York's Snickleways, which are medieval twisting passageways that take you through the old part of town and through the bars—gates through the old walls. (And bars are pubs!)

Traveling along the Rhine in Germany, we made a point to go as far as Cologne to acknowledge my passion for seeing Gothic cathedrals. Started in 1248, the Cologne Cathedral took centuries to complete. It, too, is one of the largest cathedrals in Northern Europe. It is huge, stands on a hill, and again conjures the image of this incredible building, visible for miles and days by pilgrims traveling across the country-side on foot or donkey in the 13th century. The cathedral claims to have relics of the magi in its reliquary. On a tour with a docent in the cathedral, I asked if the relics had been carbon-dated to ensure their validity, and she responded, "Of course not!" But claims of a religious relic brought pilgrims, so cathedrals had to have them, whether real or hoax.

Gothic cathedrals I have admired in other countries include Saint Barbara's Cathedral in Kutná Hora, Czech Republic, which was built in 1388, and Saint Vitus Cathedral in Prague, which was built in 1344. By the time we visited these, Richard was happy to sit on a park bench outside, notably not as enamored with Gothic architecture as I am. These Czech cathedrals were built a century later than most of those in France, England, and Germany, but the Gothic inspiration was strong enough to be carried throughout Europe. The Duomo in Florence, Italy, was later by another century (1420–1436) and is less spectacular, in my opinion, but it holds the largest dome ever constructed. Engineers today still don't understand how it could have been built and stayed intact all these centuries later.

I also appreciate some of the Gothic buildings that are not cathedrals. The style was used significantly in the Nether-lands and Belgium for government buildings and merchant centers. Just as the Dutch were leaders in great paintings that were not religious, they were also leaders in using the elements of Gothic architecture in secular buildings. We see some secular Gothic style in the US too, as in the University of Chicago buildings and also in the National Cathedral in Washington, DC. Those early designers certainly influenced architecture for centuries, but some architectural purists (such as my architecture professors in college) say medieval architecture doesn't belong in 20th-century United States.

The term *Gothic* came from the word *Goths*, who were marauders in the Dark Ages, and somehow, the critics were resistant to the massive change from Romanesque and attached this derogatory term to the new architecture. I know people often resist change, but I can't imagine how anyone could not see the beauty in the magnificent and incredibly imposing new style in the 11th century. I can understand that some people thought these towering buildings would collapse, and some did, but the fact that so many are still standing attests to their amazing engineering as well as inspiring style. As I said, I am not religious, but I certainly am inspired by the incredible architecture.

BAROQUE ARCHITECTURE

As the centuries moved on, Gothic architecture was embellished with more carving, more decorations, and fancier everything. In my opinion, that reduced the artistic integrity of the original Gothic design. The later Gothic cathedrals were more ornate than the earlier ones. As architecture continued to evolve, the style was labeled "baroque." The 16th century produced many more cathedrals, and some of the older ones were redecorated to bring them up to date. I have not made a point to visit many of these or learn the details of the differences over the centuries. I am not inspired by Renaissance church architecture, but I am often amazed by it.

I think of some of the 17th-century churches in Central and South America, for example. When I was working in Cuernavaca for a couple of weeks, my host took me to Taxco on the weekend. It is a little town hanging on the mountainside near silver mines. There are some obviously rich silver dealers in the shops around the square, but most residents are very poor, selling food in the square and eking by with tourist money. The huge church dominates the town, and the interior is covered with gold-leaf walls, altars, and statues. It is concerning that with so much poverty, the church has lavished so much expensive gilt on everything. I suppose that is similar to the extreme differences between the medieval pilgrims and the spectacular, towering stone and glass cathedrals in the 11th and 12th centuries. But somehow, it is harder to reconcile in the 20th century.

When baroque continued to add decoration, it became rococo, so extreme that it lost its integrity with the goal of just making everything fancier. A friend dubbed it "pompous baroque rococo." The epitome of this style is the cathedral La Sagrada Familia in Barcelona by architect Antoni Gaudí. It is so ornate (and continues to be built) that it generated the English word *gaudy*. Underlying the design is tall, spired Gothic. But all the design elements have been taken to the extreme. Gaudi started the building in 1883 and planned to have four towers of 400 feet each, plus a middle tower 450 feet tall. He died in 1926 with the building unfinished, but it has been continued according to his design until today. It is ostentatious and controversial and takes the Gothic elements of soaring height to the extreme. It adds so much decoration that I think it detracts from the original purpose of connecting earth with heaven.

There are numerous examples of baroque and rococo architecture around the world, often in palaces built in the 18th and 19th centuries. Some were built to outdazzle other rulers' extravagances. One such is the Dolmabahçe Palace in Istanbul, built to compete with the French Versailles. When I saw it, "pompous baroque rococo" came to mind immediately. It was the last Ottoman palace built in the late 19th century before the empire was defeated in World War I.

STAVE CHURCHES

Another ancient style of church architecture I learned about all those years ago was the stave churches of Norway. I finally got to see some firsthand on a trip to Norway in 2012. While not as awe-inspiring as Gothic cathedrals, they too are amazing. Built of wood, some have survived over eight hundred years. The Urnes Stave Church was built in 1130 and is now a UNESCO World Heritage Site. The builders were aware of the Gothic movement in the rest of Europe and used some of the same characteristics but in wood, not stone. The staves are load-bearing beams angled in the corners. The Urnes Stave Church was built on the site of an earlier church from the 11th century when Christianity was introduced to Norway.

One of the reasons they have lasted this long is because the wood was treated with pine tar, which preserved them. However, out of one thousand stave churches from medieval times, only twenty-eight still survive today. They were built by people who had become Christian, so they had some of the characteristics of most Christian churches—a nave and altar, often with a transept. One distinct difference of these stave churches is the carved animals—pagan symbols on the outside of the roofs—just in case the Christian God wasn't going to save them from the demons!

MOORISH ARCHITECTURE

Another style of architecture that I find beautiful and inspiring is Moorish design. Islam doesn't allow icons, so no sculpture of saints or images of people are allowed at all. Instead, there are elaborate designs, often carved in stone, that decorate mosques and palaces.

The Alhambra in Granada, Spain, is jaw-dropping awesome. It is a monumental complex, including three palaces built in the 14th century. The buildings are so different from Gothic cathedrals but generate wonder as well. The distinctive arches and pillars, the intricate carvings and paintings of floral and geometric motifs that decorate ceilings and walls are truly works of art. The last Moorish ruler surrendered the Alhambra to Spanish Catholic rulers in 1492. Today it is a UNESCO World Heritage Site to be maintained for future generations.

The Andalusian influence is found in Morocco as well. The Northern part of the country was the refuge for Muslims expulsed from Spain in the early 16th century, who brought the Moorish architecture. Then the Arabs from the Ottoman Empire invaded a century later and expanded the Arabian influence. The Mohammed V Mosque in Casablanca is the third-largest in the world (the larger ones are in Saudi Arabia), and while built in modern times, it uses the historical, beautiful designs of Islam. The mosque in Marrakech is the tallest building there—no building can be built taller.

The style is also used in contemporary buildings—hotels, restaurants, etc. The Museum of Contemporary Art in the capital city of Rabat is a new building with carved decorations of typical Moorish design. The mausoleum of King Mohammed V, grandfather of the present king, is an opulent example of Islamic architecture. We had dinner one evening in a kasbah that was a lovely example of the design in carved wood and tiles in a non-religious setting. The king has palaces in several cities, and they are all in characteristic Islam architecture. In Marrakech, we visited the Bahia Palace built in the 19th century by the grand vizier of the

sultan for his favorite wife. It, too, had beautiful Islamic/
Moroccan designs in the tiles, painted ceilings, and carved
wood walls. The only part of Morocco that doesn't display
this beautiful architecture and design is the southern part
in the Sahara Desert, which was settled by Berbers, who are
still the primary population there. Their art is weaving the
famous Berber carpets, which are made of wool since so
many residents are sheepherders.

Another example of Islamic architecture is the Blue Mosque
in Istanbul, built in the 16th century. It is called blue because
of the twenty thousand blue Turkish Iznik tiles covering the
interior walls. Also in Istanbul is the Hagia Sophia, a thousand years older and built originally as the world's grandest
Christian cathedral. In the 15th century, the Muslim Ottomans plastered over the Christian frescoes, and it became
a mosque. When I was there, the Christian frescoes were
uncovered as it was being restored as a museum, but just
recently, President Erdoğan has decided it must become
a mosque again. That means the ancient frescoes will be
plastered over again.

ARCHEOLOGY

As you have learned by now, I love old things—very old! The
oldest influence by people that I have seen are the Caves
of Lascaux, France. As I mentioned in chapter 5 describing road trips, we finally had the opportunity to visit these
caves. They were discovered in 1940 when some boys were
following their dog, which fell into a small opening in the
hillside. Archeologists have determined that the artwork on
the walls is from seventeen thousand years ago in Paleolithic
time! Visitors were allowed inside from 1948 until 1963

when experts realized that the carbon dioxide from so many breaths and humidity were damaging the ancient site, so they were closed to the public. It became a UNESCO World Heritage Site in 1979. A replica was built alongside it in the same hillside showing the many caverns with paintings on the walls and ceilings so visitors could again marvel at this amazing site. Just the idea that this great art was created that long ago and that it has lasted so long is incredible. We usually think that artifacts from two thousand years ago are old, and here we were, seeing art that was fifteen thousand years older!

The oldest sculptures that still exist are lions that are eight thousand years old. They are now at the entrance to the archeology museum in Istanbul, having been discovered in what is now Turkey. They have lasted this long because they are carved from basalt instead of limestone. Apparently, that many years ago, lions lived in the Middle East, so the sculptures were representational.

I was excited to finally get to see Stonehenge on a road trip in South West England. Some people say it is just a bunch of stones, but the fact that people in Neolithic times (3000 BCE) could carve these monoliths and move them into a circle is impressive. Each stone is about twelve feet high and weighs twenty-five tons! Archeologists have long studied them to try to determine their purpose, but as with so many prehistoric relics, they probably were used for religious and ceremonial rites. On another trip, our guide was able to arrange a visit at dawn, and we were allowed to actually go inside the circle, which is usually roped off so visitors can only see them from a distance. It was spectacular standing there surrounded by the monoliths because we could see the sunrise between two of them. We were there in late May, not during the summer solstice, but we could tell that in another month, the sun would be aligned with the center of the structure!

＊ ＊ ＊

On our trip to Ireland, I convinced my siblings to take a side trip to see the ancient Céide Fields near Sligo, from about 3700 BCE. They aren't as fascinated by antiquity as I am, but they also found the sites intriguing. On a hilltop with wide vistas, there is a ring of stones like Stonehenge, plus a megalithic cemetery. It was pouring rain when we were there, so we learned more about the area in the visitor center. My imagination is engaged to consider who lived there and how and why they built such permanent monuments.

We also explored the ruins of the 6th-century monastery Clonmacnoise, situated at major crossroads of the time on the River Shannon. It developed into a town, the center of religion, learning, trade, and political influence, and has attracted pilgrims for 1,500 years. It includes several churches, a castle, a tower, and the iconic Irish stone crosses. The former timber buildings are gone, but the stone ones have survived for over one thousand years.

* * *

In Mongolia, only recently has there been much archeological activity. In Khustain Nuruu National Park, we explored a Neolithic burial site with 4,000-year-old "deer stones." They are steles carved with running deer thought to carry the dead to the afterlife. Archeologists have uncovered more than five hundred of them. Some experts believe they marked the graves of important people, much like the elaborate tombs of pharaohs in Egypt.

We also visited the ruins of the ancient Mongol capital of Karakorum, founded by Genghis Khan in 1220, and a stop on the Silk Road. A new archeology museum funded by the Japanese government holds many recent discoveries from ancient civilizations here. Eighty-thousand-year-old dinosaur eggs were discovered here in the 1920s. Mongolian roads have few signs, and while driving out to this area, we got lost because neither the bus driver nor our guide was paying attention to the right road. So we lost two hours driving in the wrong direction and had to recorrect our route. Therefore, we had very little time to spend in the museum. Of course, that annoyed me since archeology museums are a favorite way to learn about ancient peoples of an area. The whole trip to Mongolia was an adventure, far off the traditional tourist track.

* * *

On the traditional border between Mongolia and China, on a trip when my niece and her family were living in China, we did the tourist thing of climbing the Great Wall. Parts were originally built in the 7th century BCE and substantially more was added in the 2nd century BCE and extended and repaired over the centuries by different dynasties. It is twenty-one thousand miles long! We only hiked about a mile of it, but that was enough to appreciate the massive construction all those years ago. It was supposed to keep out the nomadic tribes of the steppes but didn't completely succeed, because enemies breached it on occasion and invaded. Another purpose was for it to serve as border control, so duties could be charged on goods being transported on the Silk Road. It is generally considered one of the great architectural feats of history.

A truly amazing archeological site is the excavation of the Terra Cotta Army in Xi'an, China. They were first discovered in the mid-20th century by a farmer in the western part of the country. In a twenty-square-mile area, there are eight thousand soldiers, each with distinct facial features, and 170 chariots with 570 horses in a grave of China's first emperor Qin Shi Huang of the Qin dynasty in 2nd century BCE. These life-size soldiers, archers, horses, and chariots were positioned in military formation near Emperor Qin's tomb in order to protect the emperor in the afterlife. When originally unearthed, they still showed their paint and were mostly whole with just a few swords and limbs broken, still standing in rows. But exposure to the air caused the color to fade immediately, so archeologists buried some again until they could figure out how to preserve them better. Still, as you enter the enormous domed structure built to protect a section from thieves and the weather, the site is breathtaking.

The intricate carving, the detail, and the sheer number of them is just incredible. Second century BCE was the height of Greek sculpture, so it isn't surprising the Chinese sculptors of this time could create such works of art too. But as with so many amazing ancient artifacts, the skill, scope, and power of the emperor to commission such a massive project strikes me of the disparity between the common people's lives and that of emperors, pharaohs, and kings.

EGYPTIAN PYRAMIDS AND TEMPLES

Some of the oldest constructions by ancient people are the Egyptian pyramids. The oldest were built in 3000 BCE, including the Step Pyramid in Saqqara, one the largest structures ever built.

The whole area is a necropolis, which was used for 3,000 years to bury pharaohs, with much of it still unexcavated. People are allowed to climb on the Step Pyramid, but the blocks that make up the steps are so big, my stride certainly could not climb each in one step. What is amazing, as with all the ancient structures, is that these huge blocks of stone could even be moved, let alone put in place 5,000 years ago with no machinery.

Another incredible location is Giza outside of Cairo, with three pyramids, including the Great Pyramid of Cheops, which was included in the Seven Wonders of the Ancient World. Built around 2600 BCE, it is 450 feet tall. It stood as the tallest man-made structure for nearly 3,800 years until some of the spires of the Gothic cathedrals surpassed it. We were allowed to enter the third pyramid to see the burial chamber. Considering the huge size of these pyramids, it is surprising that the burial chamber is relatively small. Some have multiple passageways, either to help the dead get to the afterlife or perhaps to keep grave robbers from finding the rooms with the sarcophagus and all the gold. Much of the hieroglyphic painting on the walls has survived too.

Giza is also the location of the famous Sphinx, which was buried in sand for thousands of years.

As I have said earlier, the fact that these massive structures could be built all those years ago and last for thousands of years is in itself an exceptional accomplishment and still inspires awe. The only thing to diminish the impact of these incredible monuments is having to run the gauntlet of vendors to get from the parking lot to the monuments. We had a guard assigned to our group to ensure that we weren't bothered either by aggressive hawkers or by possible pick-pockets. Once past those, we were free to walk the desert area around those amazing sites.

On a river trip up the Nile, we also were able to explore many ancient temples. Not only are they amazing of them-selves, but the fact that many were dismantled and moved stone by stone to higher ground when the Aswan Dam was being built in 1965. Lake Nassar, one of the world's largest man-made lakes, was created by the dam which flooded the ancient land of the Nubians and would have submerged many irreplaceable monuments. Egypt's Department of Antiquities, with the help of UNESCO and many countries, embarked on a rescue project beyond the scope of anything ever before attempted.

We visited the Temples of Philae, a complex of ruins of tem-ples from the 4th century BCE, purported to be the burial site of the God Osiris. There are many other temples along the Nile that were moved to higher ground to preserve them from the rising waters. They are all amazing, especially with the paintings still intact. Our guide in Egypt was an artist and knew not only the history of all these temples but could interpret all the art and hieroglyphics on the walls, making them so much more meaningful to us. He also drew an Egyptian "alphabet" of symbols that stand for words, so we could interpret more of the hieroglyphs we were seeing.

I think the most spectacular of the rescued antiquities, and the most intact, is Abu Simbel. It comprises a mas-sive complex of temples guarded by four colossal statues of

Ramses II, each more than sixty feet high. Inside, the walls are covered with well-preserved murals depicting scenes of Queen Nefertari and her court and of King Ramses. (All over Egypt, there are statues of King Ramses II, perhaps the most egotistical of ancient rulers!) In the evening, we watched a narrated sound and light show with the facade lit up, providing an appropriately impressive view of this amazing construction.

Another area of ancient temples and tombs are the Valley of the Kings and Valley of the Queens at Luxor. We flew over in hot air balloons in the early morning, which gave us a great view of the somewhat isolated area in the desert. Much of it has only recently been excavated, buried in sand for thousands of years. Luxor is also the site of the Temple of Karnak, built by many rulers over 1,500 years, and Luxor Temple. Ramses, Tutankhamun, and even Alexander the Great built onto this massive complex. The great temple at the heart of Karnak is so big that Saint Peter's, Milan's, and Notre-Dame Cathedrals would all fit within its walls.

Most of these temples and tombs have been looted over the centuries, but magnificent paintings remain, having been protected by sand from sun and wind damage. Through this whole trip, I was enthralled by the ancient architecture, sculpture, and art treasures from the past trying to be saved for the future. Some countries have a few ancient relics, Egypt has hundreds, and with an instructive guide, one can't help but be awed by it all.

MORE ANCIENT TEMPLES

All over the Middle East are ruins of temples, some in better repair than others. Of course, Greece was the center of construction in the sixth century BCE. With so many gods, they had to have many temples to honor and worship them all. The Parthenon in Athens is the epitome of classical Greek architecture. Built in the 5th century BCE, it was dedicated to the goddess Athena. From the 6th century CE with Byzantine Christians conquering Greece, the Parthenon was stripped of its pagan symbols and was used as a Christian church until the 15th century, when the Ottomans transformed it to a mosque. I was appalled to learn that the frieze of sculptures on the front tympanum of the pediment were cut out and taken to England in the 19th century by Lord Elgin, and now, known as the Elgin Marbles, they are housed in the British Museum. There is currently an attempt by the Greeks to get their historical artifacts returned. Also on the Acropolis is the beautiful temple of the caryatids, draped female figures used as columns to hold up the pediment. After visiting the Parthenon during the day, we had dinner one evening at a rooftop restaurant across town. We had the magnificent view of the Parthenon on the Acropolis lit up by floodlights.

There are other temples throughout the country, including those in the Greek Islands, plus the Greeks built beautiful temples all over the Mediterranean area. I learned that the ones that have survived were turned into Christian churches in the common era and so were maintained. The others were either allowed to deteriorate or were intentionally torn down because they were pagan! Often the stones of the temples were reused to build churches. Sicily has many well-preserved temples, particularly in the Valley of the Temples in Agrigento, called "the most beautiful city of mortals," where there are eight Greek temples built in the 6th and 5th centuries BCE. The Temples of Concordia, the largest Doric temple ever built, and Olympian Zeus, are two of the best-preserved Greek temples in the world.

The refined architectural features of Greek temples are beautiful to look at—the proportions and the sculptured stone detail of the columns. As with the Gothic cathedrals, I prefer the clean lines of Doric or the scrolls of Ionic columns. The leaves and decorations of Corinthian columns are intriguing because they were carved from stone, but then all ancient sculpture was carved in stone! Obviously, ancient stone carvers were skilled artists. Many temples have empty niches because most of the sculptures of the gods from the temples have been moved to museums.

Sicily was on the sailing route across the Mediterranean Sea and was invaded by many armies, and so it was influenced by many cultures over the centuries. Sicilian food today incorporates Italian, of course, but also Arabic and African plus seafood, so we enjoyed the food as well as the architecture.

* * *

In Cambodia, I was enthralled by the temples at Angkor Wat. It is the largest religious monument in the world at over 402 acres. Built in the 12th century as Hindu temples, the complex was transformed into Buddhist temples in the 13th century. The architecture is considered the height of Khmer architecture, with an outer wall of 2.2 miles and three temples with towers inside. Angkor Wat (*Wat* means "temple") is the largest and best-preserved. While I thought the architecture was incredible and so different from that of the 12th century in Europe, it is the bas relief sculpture in friezes on the walls that is so amazing.

It is considered the longest linear carving in the world. Our local guide pointed out the meaning of one section of the carvings. There are three levels—the middle one representing earth, with men and women toiling in their daily lives. The upper level shows the heavenly dancers and the joys of going to heaven. And the lower level shows the horrors of hell-devils torturing people in awful, graphic ways. There are thirty-seven heavens and thirty-two hells of Hinduism depicted.

I have learned from visiting ancient temples around the world that the concept of heaven and hell are not only Christian. It is why there was so much effort by diverse civilizations to prepare people and royalty with riches especially, for the afterlife. Much effort has been made to ensure that mortals become immortal.

In addition to Angkor Wat, I also visited the recently uncovered Ta Prohm Temple, which was overgrown by huge roots of enormous kapok trees and vines. I only had two days in Cambodia after a trip to Thailand, so I didn't have time to study all the carvings on the temple, let alone explore the other temples in the area. I have wanted to return to Cambodia ever since that visit, and it is still on my list.

RUINS OF ANCIENT CITIES

Some of the most incredible archeological finds I have visited have been ruins of cities built two or more millennia ago. Present-day Turkey is a treasure trove of sites that boggle the mind to see the advanced architecture and living conditions of ordinary people in the centuries before the common era. The most notable I think is Ephesus, near present-day Kuşadası, perhaps the world's best-preserved ancient city. It was the provincial capital of Asia in Roman times, with a population of 250,000. There are ruins of the Temple of Diana, one of the Seven Wonders of the Ancient World, and the Temple of Hadrian with the head of Medusa to keep away evil spirits. There is the enormous theater that holds twenty-four thousand people and is still used today, and the two-story Library of Celsus, which once held twelve thousand ancient scrolls.

We walked down the main street called the Sacred Way, with ruins of rich people's stone houses, including an ingenious water and sewer system beneath the marble pavement. This, of course, is where Saint Paul wrote one of his epistles to the Ephesians. I learned that the reason he was jailed here was not because he was Christian, but that he was preaching against worshiping the Goddess Diana, and the local merchants were losing money from not selling Diana statues, so they wanted Paul out of the way.

The advanced city from 2,500 years ago made me wonder what happened? How did civilization go from this level of sophisticated engineering and construction, government, and luxury to the depths of the Dark Ages? Some of it was the fall of the Roman Empire to the Mongols and Vandals, and some of it was intentional destruction of pagan civilizations by Christian zealots and the distrust of science by the church. Add to those factors endless wars that damaged everything of value and still do today. I am saddened that I have not been able to visit Syria before all the destruction of their great ancient civilization and the horrendous suffering of the Syrian people.

We also visited Troy, which is no longer on the sea because of the silting over five thousand years. Archeologists have uncovered nine levels of Trojan civilizations. The Iliad made it seem that Troy was a myth, but evidence shows otherwise. There are excavations of amazing sites all through the Mediterranean coast of Turkey. We saw Lycian rock tombs, the only known remnant of this ancient civilization, a huge Roman theater with the stage and backstage areas still intact, and a 6th-century Byzantine monastery. In Antalya, there is a great archeological museum, which houses much of the sculptures removed from so many ruins to be preserved from the weather and thieves.

* * *

Petra, Jordan, is the most amazing ancient city I have seen. Not only is it jaw-dropping awesome, but even more so because you approach on foot through a slot canyon (called a Siq) of about a mile. You are walking on sand with steep, narrow canyon walls with only a glimmer of light far in the distance.

Then all of a sudden, the canyon ends, and you step out in front of a multistory building carved in the red stone wall. It is facing a street with the remains of colonnades, many buildings, and a huge open-air theater. There are five hundred royal tombs carved in the mountains of rock. All this was the civilization of the Nabataeans from the 4th century BCE to the 1st century CE. The buildings show influences of the Assyrians, who also used tombs carved in the mountainsides, but the columns on the first building you see, called the Treasury, have Hellenistic architectural features.

The Nabataeans became wealthy because Petra was on the trade route from the Dead Sea to the Red Sea, an oasis in the desert for the camel caravans. The Treasury is so well-preserved because it is protected by the rock canyons in front of it. The more open parts of the ancient city are less well preserved but still fascinating. You can see remnants of their engineered water system carved in the canyon wall that brought water from the mountains to the town. No one knows why the Nabataeans disappeared, and in fact, Petra was unknown until the 19th century, when it was "discovered" and is now a national park of Jordan.

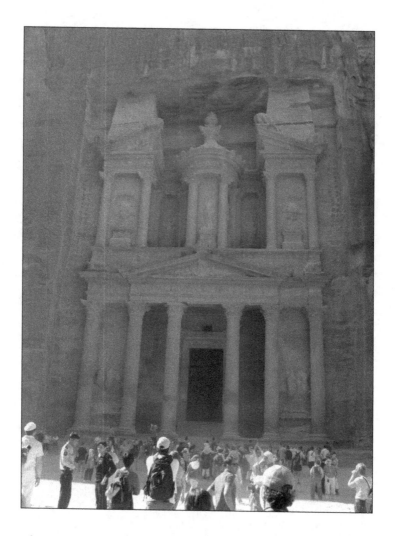

Also in Jordan, in Amman, we explored the ruins of Jerash, called the "Pompei of the East" because it is so well preserved from the time of Alexander the Great in the early centuries of the common era. It is the largest Roman site outside of Italy with colonnaded streets, temples, and an amphitheater. Between Amman and Petra is the 12th-century Ajloun Castle of Saladin, built to fend off the crusaders. It even withstood Richard the Lionheart but fell to Mongols in the 13th century.

* * *

Of course, there are Roman ruins all around the Mediterranean area and beyond: from Morocco on the western end
to Jordan and Turkey in the east; and France, Sicily, Italy;
of course, Bulgaria; and even as far as England. I have seen,
and in some cases sat in, Roman amphitheaters still usable
after two thousand years, and they still have amazing acous-
tics. We watched chariot races in the Roman amphitheater
in Amman, Jordan, learned about the levels and rituals of
gladiators in the amphitheater in Arles, France, and visited
the Roman baths of marble in Bath, England. You can walk
in the amphitheater in Sofia, Bulgaria, which was used until
recently. Most of the original buildings from the Roman
Empire in present-day Rome have been buried over the centuries and since excavated. It is interesting that residents
today just live with the ruins and take them for granted after
two thousand years.

The most amazing city in Italy that has been excavated
is Pompei, which was buried by the eruption of Mount
Vesuvius in 79 CE. Because of the ash that suffocated the
inhabitants and caused sudden death, the archeological site
is a treasure of information about how they lived. Marble
floors and frescoes still exist in what were lavish homes,
and all sorts of artifacts have been uncovered. The most
incredible finds were the bodies entombed in the ash, which
decayed and left hardened voids that archaeologists used to
make plaster casts of often gruesome figures in their final
moments of life. These insights into how people lived, and
in this case, died, are what I find fascinating about archeological sites.

***

An intriguing city from the 17th century and still lived in is Ait-Ben-Haddou in Morocco. Built completely of red rock on a red rock mountainside, it was a stop on the caravan route from the desert to Marrakech. Ait gained fame in the 20th century as the site of films and TV shows, such as *Game of Thrones*, *Lawrence of Arabia*, and *Gladiator*. A UNESCO World Heritage Site, it is considered a classic example of Southern Moroccan architecture (desert Berber rather than Arab or Muslim in the North).

City centers of narrow streets and passageways are kasbahs; countryside spots like Ait-Ben-Haddou are ksars. They are filled with vendors and shops selling everything imaginable. We had lunch with a family there and watched a kind of pizza being baked in a communal outdoor oven, and then we had a picnic in a nearby field. The family spoke no English, so our guide translated. The kids performed a song for us, so one of our group taught the whole group the Hokey Pokey. The adults as well as the kids and our small group all got in a circle and learned quickly what it meant to "put your right hand in," etc., and had a great laugh.

OLD CIVILIZATIONS IN THE NEW WORLD

Some of the ruins of ancient Mayan cities in Belize and Guatemala in Central America are as old and fascinating as those I have been describing. Many of the temples have relatively recently been excavated, and some are only partially so to this day. There are also some pyramid-shaped hills that archeologists suspect have more buried pyramids. Unlike the Middle East, where monuments were buried by sand, here they are hidden and overgrown by jungles.

Some sites, like the Jaguar Temple, were occupied for thousands of years, from perhaps 1500 BCE to 1500 CE. Unlike the smooth sides of most of the Egyptian pyramids, the huge stones of these were built as steps. This one was forgotten and hard to find, so the Spaniards didn't invade the area.

Tikal in Guatemala is a large complex with ruins of local residences as well as the sacred shrines. The oldest section is from 350 BCE. There are 185 steps to the top of the Grand Pyramid, which, along with two other temples, was designed with astronomical alignment for the summer solstice, the equinoxes, and winter solstice. It is impressive how complex their understanding of astronomy was and how that influences all these buildings.

As I wrote about in chapter 5, I have also had the opportunity to explore some ruins of ancient cities in the American Southwest. Best known and best-preserved is Mesa Verde at the corners of what are now Colorado, New Mexico, and Utah. These pueblos were built into the mountainside in the 12th century. Mesa Verde is on the same longitude as Chaco Canyon, which is 135 miles south in New Mexico. Archeologists believe the site was abandoned because the big game was overhunted and the mesa deforested, followed by a drought. Mesa Verde was discovered in the 1880s and was plundered until it was made a national park in 1906. I was surprised that the park management allowed visitors to climb the ladders and walk through some of the buildings just as the cliff dwellers did.

A similar ancient Anasazi city was built at Chaco Canyon, New Mexico. It is not on a cliff like Mesa Verde but has ruins of extensive and unique architecture, such as stone "great houses" and a network of roads. It was a thriving, complex community one thousand years ago. Like my reaction to the advanced civilizations of two thousand years ago, I wondered, "Why did it end?" As with Mesa Verde, the assumption is that environmental degradation made it necessary for the residents to leave all this behind. Chaco Canyon is a National Historic Park, but I was surprised that I had not heard of it before and was fascinated by the complexity of the site and how intact some of the buildings still are. There are so few man-made places in the US that are this old, we tend not to expect such. A revolutionary-era home in the Eastern US is only two to three hundred years old, and in many European cities, that is common. It is the 800-year-old buildings or the 1,000-year-old churches that get attention. So here in the southwestern desert, we have a whole civilization from one thousand years ago that has disappeared, leaving a remarkably engineered site for us to explore.

As I write this, the Trump administration has quietly, under cover of the COVID-19 pandemic, offered leases to oil companies to drill and frack in Chaco Canyon. Of course, the native peoples who live in the area and revere the site of their ancestors are vehemently opposed to this infraction of their rights. This is patently illegal to do in a National Historic Park, but he and his oil industry cabinet leaders disregard laws and hope they can get away with this irreversible damage. Once again, the conservation organizations will try to stop them in court. I hope it happens before they ruin this irreplaceable monument.

Much as I am fascinated by archeology and the civilizations

and peoples it represents, I learned early in my life that I could not actually be an archeologist. In the 1970s, I led my troop of Senior Girl Scouts on a wilderness camping trip to the Girl Scout National Center West in the Wind River Range near Ten Sleep, Wyoming. One of the explorations available to girls there was an archeological dig directed by an archeologist from the University of Wyoming. There is a natural rock amphitheater in the mountain that had been used by Native American tribes over the centuries, and the dig was set up to carefully sift through the dirt layers to see what could be found. We spent a couple of days doing so, and found mostly remains of fires that had been built there long ago. It is tedious work that requires much patience and attention. A good experience for the girls and for me, but it reinforced my decision to explore sites after the scientists had done their work to marvel at their findings, but not to be the finder!

ARTIFACTS

Most ancient artifacts that still exist are in museums. My favorites are always archeological museums that hold the sculpture and other artifacts from the archeological sites I love to explore. The Istanbul Archeological Museum was established in the 19th century after the leaders had visited the Louvre in Paris. It has huge collections from most of the excavations in Turkey, as well as Greek and Roman artifacts from the expanse of the Ottoman Empire. The sarcophagus of Alexander the Great is there, as well as statues removed from ancient temples and all sorts of cultural items from pottery to gold jewelry and coins to everyday items, only thousands of years old!

* * *

The Museum of Egyptian Antiquities in Cairo is an old, poorly maintained building but with a treasure trove inside. They are in the process of building a huge new building outside of Cairo, but it wasn't open yet when we visited. The most famous items in the museum are the sarcophagus of King Tutankhamun and all the luxurious items that were buried with him. His tomb from 2,500 years ago was hidden, so it was not robbed over all those years. It was excavated in the early 20th century, and everything was moved to the museum for preservation. I saw the King Tut exhibit that traveled to the US years ago, but it was especially impressive to see it (in spite of the crowds) in Cairo, close to where the tomb was found.

The National Archeological Museum of Athens is one of the most important museums in the world that houses ancient Greek art. The Greeks were such prolific sculptors that there are Greek statues and artifacts in museums around the world. It is so impressive to see them in close proximity to the excavations and ruins where they originated. The museum also has an extensive exhibit of Greek pottery, where visitors can learn the evolution of painting over the centuries.

The British Museum in London was the first free national museum in the world, built in 1759. Because the British Empire had such a far reach, the museum acquired millions of artifacts and building parts from around the world. Many are fascinating, but I am less impressed when items have been bought or forcibly removed from their origins to be displayed in the museum than when they are saved in the locale or country of origin.

Another such museum that has preserved important antiquities is the Oriental Institute Museum at the University of Chicago. It is where I first saw preserved Egyptian mummies, so there is educational value to have them in the US, but I find it so much more awesome to see things like this in their original environment.

Likewise, the Louvre in Paris has amazing collections of paintings and sculptures from many cultures, but it is overwhelming because it is so extensive. The best way to appreciate what is there is to take a personal tour with a guide in the evening after regular hours. Then you can request the particular art you most want to see and get knowledgeable commentary too. In Paris, I much prefer the Musée d'Orsay, which focuses on the Impressionists, or the Musée de l'Orangerie, which houses a collection of Monet's paintings.

The Rijksmuseum in the Netherlands is also impressive. After so many centuries of painting the Madonna and Child in Europe, the art of the Renaissance broke free in the Netherlands and Belgium with secular painting—Rembrandt painting wealthy merchants; Bruegel painting skaters and other scenes of normal activity. Except for these exceptional museums, I tend not to go to art museums in most countries I visit. They all love to show off their French Impressionists, Dutch masters, or Italian religious paintings. I much prefer to see the art of the country I am visiting. In Rabat, Morocco, for example, it was enlightening to see the history of Islamic art in a new museum.

In addition to archeology museums, other museums that make an impact on me are those that show difficult or awful periods in history. The Apartheid Museum in Soweto,

South Africa, has mostly photographs that tell the story of the cruel impact that the apartheid had on the population. Soweto was a community of one million, the largest black city during apartheid, which is still segregated and poor. Also, the United States Holocaust Memorial Museum in Washington, DC, takes you through the rise of Hitler in Germany in the 1930s through Nazi rule and World War II. You know they are well done when the images and artifacts cause emotion and even anger in the viewers, as these two do. The museum in Caen, Normandy, has the best exhibit I have seen of the Normandy invasion and D-Day. They show two films simultaneously on the screen with footage of the Germans on the morning of D-Day at the same time when the Allies were landing on the beaches. It shows the horror, heroism, personal impact, and outcomes in people's lives.

One of the other benefits of local museums is that they often have excellent museum shops, which is where I buy some of the historical pottery for my collection.

POTTERY

Besides architecture, pottery is my next favorite medium for artistic expression. I personally learned how to throw pots just well enough to appreciate good quality when I see it, but not good enough to create anything of quality. I find that most civilizations from antiquity to the present needed pottery and developed items that were both practical and representative of their culture and locale. I am not a shopper when I travel, but I do try to acquire a sample of the pottery of the culture.

My favorite plate and bowl are reproductions of the pottery found in Petra, Jordan. There were enough shards for a contemporary potter and chemist to analyze how it was made over two thousand years ago. It is made of red clay, which is the soil of the area, and the reason Petra is called the Red City. The pottery is very thin and delicate-looking but strong, with decorations painted on with darker red clay. You know when things were functional, they had to be tough. Of course, I just have most of my pieces in a collection, not to cook in or eat from.

* * *

In Nigeria, I purchased the opposite kind of pottery. It is thick and heavy. We watched the women make pots, starting with a lump of clay on the ground, then bending over and walking around it to shape it. Not only did they not have a wheel, but they didn't even own a table or workbench, and there was no kiln! Their pots were fired in a charcoal fire on the ground near where the pots were made. The decorations were scratched into the surface. More unique, I bought a stand for it carved from ebony with three legs representing the three tribes—Hausa, Igbo, and Yoruba—that united to form present-day Nigeria.

* * *

Perhaps the most unusual purpose of a piece of pottery I have is the Canopic jar from Egypt. The jars were glazed with figures on the lid and buried with the body to hold the mummified organs! Of course, mine is a reproduction bought in the museum store of the archeology museum in Egypt.

* * *

The Greeks in antiquity used pottery vessels primarily to store, transport, and drink liquids such as wine, oil, and water. Smaller pots were used as containers for perfumes and unguents. Because fired pottery is long-lasting, much of what we know about Greek art is because so many pieces still exist. There are many shapes, depending on the intended use, as well as scenes depicting normal and special events in Greek life. The pieces from as long ago as 1000 BCE have primarily geometric designs. Later pieces depicted stories and used human and animal figures, including mythical griffins, sirens, and gorgons. The older pottery used shiny black glaze, and later pottery had black figures on red backgrounds. The piece I have is a replica of the old black figures on cream, with a black background. It is amazing how much Greek pottery still exists and is in museums all over the world. I have a tiny amphora urn from Turkey, a replica of those used for wine found in the excavations of 2,000-year-old cities.

* * *

An ancient pottery still made today is Australian Aboriginal Dream Weaver patterns. Made of terra-cotta, they have painted stylized Australian animals, snakes, and dots. Native American pottery has also been made continuously for hundreds of years. Each group had its historical style, and they continue to create beautiful pieces today. When I was traveling in the Southwest with my friend Liz, we visited some Navaho pueblos, and I bought two signed pots by potters from the Acoma Pueblo. Liz is a potter and creates beautiful contemporary pots, and she has also studied the indigenous pottery, so it was good to have her insights as we explored Utah and New Mexico. I also have a black-on-black piece from the Taos Pueblo. In Mexico, there are different artistic styles in different states. I have a beautiful large plate from Jalisco with the natural terra-cotta painted with subtle rust-and-gray patterns.

Each culture and country seems to have its own styles of pottery, some from ancient times and some contemporary. Bulgarian pottery is ceramic with a distinctive geometric pattern, typically in blue and yellow. Traditional Slovakian ceramics have floral patterns in yellow and white, sometimes with a bit of red, which represents blood. In the hill towns of Northern Italy, each town has its own signature product. One sells everything made of alabaster, another painted kitchenware, another olive dishes, etc. I learned that if I saw something I liked, I needed to buy it there because I wouldn't find it again in the next town. The Netherlands, of course, is known for Delft, well-known blue-and-white ceramics. I have a tulip vase, representing both the pottery and the trademark of Holland.

China is known for its handmade cloisonné. We visited a factory where women were decorating pots and vases with fine wire designs and then delicately adding enamel in bright colors. I prefer terra-cotta or natural colors, so I asked if I could purchase a piece that was unfinished—clay with the wire design before the enamel was added. They weren't sure what I was asking, so my niece's daughter, who was studying Mandarin in school, helped explain what I wanted. No one had asked for an unfinished piece before, so they had to come up with a price a bit lower than the finished enameled ware.

In Fes, Morocco, we visited a contemporary ceramics factory. We were able to watch all the steps of the pottery being made, from the man in the pit kneading the clay and water with his hands and feet; to the expert potter throwing the bowls, lids, and tagines; to the artists painting the designs; to the firing. Every family in Morocco has several tagines—clay bases with a conical lid for steaming meat or vegetables. Our meals in restaurants and riads (inns) were served either in individual tagines or sometimes in a large one for the table. I decided to buy tagines as gifts for the cooks in my family!

In Argentina, the calabash that I bought is actually carved from a gourd and decorated. It is used to drink maté tea. From Fiji, too, the vase I have is not made of clay but is carved from wood, so I don't put water in it. Instead, I fill it with silk flowers.

OTHER INDIGENOUS CRAFTS

When in Tonga in the Southern Pacific, instead of pottery, I bought a large wall hanging made of tapa cloth, their traditional craft. It is made of levels of bark glued together with graphic designs painted with natural colors.

Mongolian crafts are typically painted on leather. The distinctive style has camels, deer, and other stylized animals. Sometimes they include people scattered on the painting, sort of stacked, without perspective. It fits into the category of primitive painting, which is representative of the culture.

From Cambodia, instead of a pot, I have a panel molded in plaster that is a replica of some of the heavenly dancers depicted on the bas relief of the temples. I was pleased to have from the Alhambra in Spain, two panels that are replicas of the Islamic tracery carved in stone in the mosques.

Guatemala is known for its fabrics, especially multicolored, beautiful textiles for the table and clothes. I enjoy negotiating with vendors since it's part of the culture in Central America. I get a fair price while ensuring that the seller benefits too. That is so different from the blatantly dishonest vendors in Cairo, where they offer a price, you accept, and then when the package is wrapped and handed to you, the price suddenly goes up ten times or more.

While I was running my company, we collected fabric art from each of the countries where we worked. I have a panel of Dream Weavers art from Australia, a scroll with Chinese characters saying "path through life" aka career, a tapestry of part of the Bayeux Tapestry from Belgium, a primitive painting on leather of a Mexican village, a panel with silk stitching from Hong Kong, and a woven hunting scene from England. They hung in my office until I retired; now they hang in my home office.

I treasure my collection of pottery and crafts for their variety and beauty, but especially because each piece reminds me of the culture of a country I have visited. I just decided to count these for the first time and found that I have sixty-two terra-cotta or ceramic items, representing most of the sixty countries I have explored on six continents. No indigenous crafts on Antarctica!

"When I'm working on a problem, I never think about beauty. I think only how to solve the problem. But when I have finished, if the solution is not beautiful, I know it is wrong."

—BUCKMINSTER FULLER

AFTERWORD

"You cannot discover new oceans unless you have the courage to lose sight of the shore."

—ANDRÉ GIDE

I need to have challenge in my life, as you can see from reading this book. Over the years as a career coach, I would ask clients what motivated them. Another question was, "What is important to you in your work?" These questions brought out answers about values and what we called "anchors." Some people need security, for whom risk is not something they take willingly. Others prefer autonomy or need to demonstrate competence. Some, like me, need challenge. I needed it in my work, and as a retiree, I need it in my life. I get it from travel, from new learning, not from books but from experiences. I am not content to stay at home with a routine. During this COVID-19 pandemic, I have had my travel curtailed, but I still have plans for the future. I had a trip planned to Croatia and the Balkans in the fall, which I had to cancel. Europe doesn't even allow Americans in right now. But I am not ready to change my direction yet. I see the present as another challenge!

I have shared my challenges and experiences with you in these chapters. From sailing to skiing to the wonders of nature to countries' personalities to my fascination with architecture and archeology. I hope you have enjoyed some of these experiences vicariously. I also hope I have inspired you to seek your own experiences, to break away from the status quo to seek those experiences that fill your soul and give you energy for more. What are the places and adventures on your bucket list? What have you done that inspires you to do more?

There are other places high on my list to experience—Machu Picchu, the Easter Island, the Amazon. In the other direction and temperature: Iceland, Greenland, and the Svalbard Islands above the Arctic Circle in Norway. While I have not climbed Mount Everest, I have climbed and skied my share of mountains. While I have not scuba dived in the depths of the ocean, I have snorkeled all the barrier reefs. While I have not kayaked Class V rapids, I have rafted rapids in the Grand Canyon and other whitewater. While I have not raced in America's Cup, I have captained my own sailboat in several 330-mile Chicago-Mackinac races. I get my need for challenge met at my own pace, somewhat modified as I have aged, but not keeping me from seeking new challenges and new experiences. Challenges aren't always physical. As I shared in chapter 6, some of those challenges were how to see and experience the evolution of Gothic architecture in Europe or the challenge of understanding different cultures, as I wrote about in chapter 4.

It has been fun writing this compilation of my experiences and adventures, reliving them even while I look forward to more. While many experiences are now in the wake of my life's voyage, I will run out of years before I run out of adventures to experience.

"Live life like a river trip. You pack and plan and prepare the best you can. And even though you don't know everything that will happen downstream, you launch."

—ANONYMOUS

ACKNOWLEDGMENTS

Throughout all my adventure-traveling years, I have had wonderful companions who share my interests and motivation to be actively involved. My friend Wendy Davis is intrepid in challenging or less-than-hospitable environments. She initiated several of the trips I wrote about in this book—Nigeria, South Africa, Mongolia, and Provence, and she joined me on adventures in the Galápagos, Costa Rica, the Netherlands, Spain, and Portugal, Southern Italy, Sicily, Turkey, Jordan, and the garden tour of England. The only adventure I know of that she didn't relish was zip-lining in Costa Rica!

My sons Steen and Michael are sailors and skiers who have invited me and joined me on adventures on oceans and mountains, and who share my love of France. They encourage me to continue my travel adventures around the world.

Other traveling friends and family have joined me in areas where we share adventurous interests: Barb Cragan on trips to New Zealand, Egypt, and Morocco; my brother Richard Wright and sister-in-law Carol Felsing in Ireland, Mexico, and New Mexico; my sister Betty Bennett in China, Spain, Portugal, Guatemala, Honduras, Ireland, the Bahamas, and Canada; my friend Liz Solem, who helped me explore the American Southwest and Italy; and my friend Ellyn Lanz, who skied with us for years at Vail and explored European ski areas with me, as well as many of my ski trips in the US.

All of these supportive friends and family have kept me traveling and seeking adventure after I lost my husband, Bill, of forty years, and then my partner for eight years, Richard. Having such wonderful friends and family to share adventures makes them all the more rewarding.

I also thank the editors and advisors at Scribe Media for their advice and hand-holding to get my manuscript and photos into a published book!

ABOUT THE AUTHOR

PEGGY SIMONSEN has always been a trailblazer. She started a career development consulting firm, Career Directions Inc. in 1979. At the time, the only career advising was happening in schools, but she knew from work at a community college that adults were very much in need of career help. She coached women who were returning to work after a hiatus as homemakers, professionals who found they were in the wrong field, and employees who wanted advice on advancing within their organization. Trained as an educator, she initiated career management workshops for corporations.

Initially, companies wanted employees to take more responsibility for their own development. As the vice president of an old-line company said in introducing their career management program, "We said you would have a job for life, but we didn't say it would be the same job." In the 1990s, after a decade of layoffs, the corporate issue became, "How can we keep people?" She added programs to show managers how they could better develop their employees.

In addition to her development systems, Peggy published many articles and two books, *Promoting a Development Culture in Your Organization* and *Career Compass, Navigating Your Career in the 21st Century*, both by Davies-Black Publishers. She has a BS from the University of Minnesota and a MA from Northwestern University.

After retiring from a demanding career, following the death of her husband of forty years, Peggy committed her energy to her lifelong interests: skiing, sailing, nature, and traveling, often merging them. She is a board member and former President of Citizens for Conservation, an organization in Barrington, Illinois, whose mission is "Saving living space for living things through protection, restoration, and stewardship of land, conservation of natural resources, and education." She currently chairs their Community Education and Grants committees. She has restored her yard in Palatine, Illinois, with over two hundred species of native plants.

Her two sons live on each coast, so visiting them and her granddaughter also requires travel. She shares adventures with them there, too.